*Studies in Victorian
Life and Literature*

A WORLD OF POSSIBILITIES

ROMANTIC IRONY
IN VICTORIAN LITERATURE

Clyde de L. Ryals

Ohio State University Press
Columbus

Library of Congress Cataloging-in-Publication Data

Ryals, Clyde de L., 1928–
    A world of possibilities : romantic irony in Victorian literature /
Clyde de L. Ryals.
        p.   cm. – (Studies in Victorian life and literature)
    Includes bibliographical references.
    ISBN 0–8142–0522–4 (alk. paper)
    1. English literature—19th century—History and criticism.
2. Romanticism—Great Britain—History—19th century. 3. Irony in
literature. I. Title. II. Series.
PR468.R65R94   1990
820.9'18'09034—dc20   90–35593
                                                                  CIP

Printed in the U.S.A.

9   8   7   6   5   4   3   2   1

For HSR

Superlative actors! how noble
the play, how splendid
your costume, how lofty
your role!

St. Hildegard of Bingen
(trans. Barbara Newman)

CONTENTS

ACKNOWLEDGMENTS

Portions of this book have been previously published. Most of chapter 1 appeared in *ELH* (Winter 1987–88); parts of chapter 3 in *Studies in Browning and His Circle* (1986) and the *Journal of Narrative Literature* (Winter 1987); most of chapter 4 in *Victorian Poetry* (Spring–Summer 1988); parts of chapter 6 in the *Tennyson Research Bulletin* (1990); and most of chapter 7 in *Nineteenth-Century Literature* (September 1988). I thank the editors of these journals for their kind permission to reprint this material.

In addition, portions of the book were delivered as lectures: at West Virginia University (October 1985); the Conference on Narrative Poetics, Ohio State University (April 1986); the University of Münster (May 1987); the Modern Language Association in New Orleans (December 1988); and the Graduate Center of the City University of New York (May 1989). I am grateful to my hosts on these occasions. I should like especially to thank John Stasny of West Virginia University and Kurt Tetzeli von Rosador of the University of Münster for their generous hospitality when I appeared at their universities.

INTRODUCTION
An Image of the Age

After forty years of revolutions and revolutionary wars it had become apparent at the beginning of the Victorian period that the nineteenth century was to be characterized as a period of change. It was in fact the one subject on which even the most contentious persons could agree. Writing on "The Spirit of the Age" in 1831, John Stuart Mill described his as "an age of change," "the conviction [being] already not far from universal, that the times are pregnant with change." Elaborating on Mill's observation in the last decade of the century, Walter Pater noted that "the entire modern theory" of change had become "a commonplace."[1] In sum, the idea of change informed all vital thought of the Victorian age: for example, the philosophy of T. H. Green and F. H. Bradley, the geology of Charles Lyell and William Chambers, the biology of Charles Darwin and T. H. Huxley, the theology of clergymen so diverse as John Henry Newman and Benjamin Jowett, and, in a very radical way, the literary efforts of the best writers of the time.

During the early part of the period, commentators spoke of it as "an age of transition," from a time of certainty and accepted values to a time of which one knew not what. As Carlyle observed in *Sartor Resartus,* the Old Mythus had disappeared and the New Mythus had not been revealed. For many the recognition that

1

theirs was an age of transition was a fearful thing. "We live in an age of visible transition," Edward Bulwer Lytton wrote in his appraisal of the spirit of the age in 1833. "To me such epochs appear . . . the times of greatest unhappiness to our species." "It is an awful moment," Frederick Robertson said a few years later, "when the soul begins . . . to feel the nothingness of many of the traditionary opinions which have been received with implicit confidence, and in that horrible insecurity begins also to doubt whether there be any thing to believe at all."[2] Where many were made anxious by change, others were of a different disposition. Writing to his future wife in 1846, Robert Browning said: "The cant is, that 'an age of transition' is the melancholy thing to contemplate and delineate—whereas the worst things of all to look back on are times of comparative standing still, rounded in their impotent completeness."[3] Still others could be of two minds in contemplating their age. In "Locksley Hall" Alfred Tennyson viewed the time moving in exhilarating fashion "down the ringing grooves of change," whereas in "Locksley Hall Sixty Years After" he saw retrogression as the inevitable concomitant of progress.

If it is a time when "nothing is fixed, nothing is appointed," the liberal congregational theologian James Baldwin Brown said, one must adopt an attitude of skepticism about all things. "We are growing . . . more sceptical in the proper sense of the word," wrote Henry Sidgwick:

> we suspend our judgement much more than our predeces-
> sors . . . : we see that there are many sides to many questions:
> the opinions that we do hold we hold more at arm's length: we
> can imagine how they appear to others, and can conceive
> ourselves not holding them. We are . . . gaining in impartiality
> and comprehensiveness of sympathy.

This was entirely proper, according to the scientist John Tyndall, for "there are periods when the judgement ought to remain in suspense, the data on which a decision might be based being absent."[4] If there were certainties few or none, at least there was a world of possibilities.

Suspended judgment dictated by the perception that various and even contradictory views might be alike true—this was the posture that the thinking individual was forced to assume in a world of change; and basically, as philosophers and literary critics came to understand, it was an ironic stance. The historian and ecclesiastic Connop Thirlwall observed this in 1833 when addressing himself to a kind of irony dependent not upon local effects but made identical with a cosmic view. Noting that in the *Antigone* Sophocles impartially presented two equal and opposite points of view, he remarked that irony may reside in the attitude of an impartial observer or, more precisely, in the situation observed:

> There is always a slight cast of irony in the grave, calm,
> respectful attention impartially bestowed by an intelligent judge
> on two contending parties, who are pleading their causes before
> him with all the earnestness of deep conviction, and of excited
> feeling. What makes the contrast interesting is, that the right
> and the truth lie on neither side exclusively: that there is no
> fraudulent purpose, no gross imbecility of intellect, on either:
> but both have plausible claims and specious reasons to alledge,
> though each is too much blinded by prejudice or passion to do
> justice to the views of his adversary. For there the irony lies not
> in the demeanor of the judge, but is deeply seated in the case
> itself, which seems to favour each of the litigants, but really
> eludes them both.

The most interesting conflicts are not, Thirlwall says, those in which one side is obviously right, as when good is pitted against evil. For

> this case . . . seems to carry its own final decision in itself. But
> the liveliest interest arises when by inevitable circumstances,
> characters, motives, and principles are brought into hostile

collision, in which good and evil are so inextricably blended on each side, that we are compelled to give an equal share of our sympathy to each, while we perceive that no earthly power can reconcile them; that the strife must last until it is extinguished with at least one of the parties, and yet that this cannot happen without the sacrifice of something which we should wish to preserve.[5]

The kind of irony that Thirlwall describes—suspended judgment required by the indeterminacy of the case—is that now known as romantic irony. Romantic irony has not often been associated with literature in English. To critics in England and America it has seemed foreign, something made in Germany, for which there was little market in English-speaking countries. Recent critical studies, however, have helped to domesticate the term,[6] although even yet it does not enjoy widespread usage because of a lack of common understanding as to its meaning. As Lilian Furst observes, romantic irony almost seems to elude definition (p. 225).

It is important to note, in the first place, that romantic irony is unlike the local ironies that are rhetorical, polemical, satirical, and parodistic. Its purpose is not to persuade, amuse, or ridicule but, rather, to question certainties and present possibilities. It is essentially philosophical and is a response to the problem of contradictions in life that are perceived as irreconcilable. It first assumed a prominent position in European thought and literature at the close of the eighteenth century. In spite of its name, however, romantic irony is not to be associated exclusively with the Romantic period, although critics of English literature have discussed it mainly in connection with Romantic writing.

For an understanding of romantic irony we can do no better than to go to its first and foremost theoretician, the late-eighteenth and early-nineteenth-century German philosopher Friedrich von Schlegel. As he conceived it, romantic irony is rooted in the problem of the self in German idealism. How, for example, is the finite ego related to the Infinite or Absolute Ego? How may the realms of the relative and the absolute be brought together? Schlegel's answer was to posit both the finite and the infinite as a process: the essence of reality is not *being,* a substance in itself, but *becoming,* a process. In the fertile abundance of the phenomenal world, "an infinitely teeming chaos,"[7] all is change: an entity becomes something so as to become something else, is created so as to be de-created, is formed so as to be transformed. Thus everything is simultaneously both itself and not itself in that it is in the process of becoming something else: *a* is not only *a* but also *a becoming b,* and *b* is not only *b* but also *b becoming c,* and so on ad infinitum. This is the basic paradox of romantic irony, which Schlegel defined as "the form of paradox" and as "everything simultaneously great and good" (*L* 48, *KA* 2:153). There can be, as the most advanced Victorian authors came to perceive, no certainty in this world of flux because there is no stability, the only constant being change itself without *telos.*

Infinity, in Schlegel's view, is an ever-growing center of finite expressions, and finitude is a momentarily limited infinity. Reality is, accordingly, an interplay between the finite and the infinite. Ontologically the finite can never encompass the infinite, because an exhaustless fund of life constantly develops itself amidst the ever-flowing vital energy of nature. Psychologically the individual experiences the tension caused by the desire for order and coherence (*being,* on the one hand) and chaos and freedom (*becoming,* on the other) as a conflict between power and love. Epistemologically man can never attain full consciousness, an infinite self; any theoretical formulation or system of reality that he makes can be only an approximation, which ultimately must be transcended. Morally the recognition of the inadequacy of a specific formulation or system stimulates the dissatisfaction that urges the individual and the race toward evolution into ever-higher states or conditions of consciousness.

Romantic irony finds a literary mode correspondent to this world view in what Schlegel calls "progressive, universal poetry (*Universalpoesie*)," "romantic poetry" (*A* 116, *KA* 2:182) or "transcendental poetry" (*A* 238, *KA* 2:204). As "a *representation of the Universe*" (*KA* 18:213, frag. 219), it is infinite and free, forever "in the state of becoming"; it is "a mirror of the whole circumambient world, an image of the age" (*A* 116). Having its "real homeland" in philosophy (*L* 42, *KA* 2:152), it is a combination of poetry and philosophy, science and art (*L* 115, *KA* 2:161).

Since no one literary genre can accommodate this fusion, all genres are therefore to be combined. For the aim of *Universalpoesie* is not "merely to reunite all the separate species of poetry and put poetry in touch with philosophy and rhetoric" but also to "mix and fuse poetry and prose, inspiration and criticism, the poetry of art and the poetry of nature" (*A* 116, *KA* 2:182). It can therefore be a poem, a drama, a novel, or some intermixture thereof. Taking all forms, modes, styles, and genres for its expression, it will employ, *inter alia,* fragments, differing perspectives, critical comments, disruptions of cause and effect, and confessional interpolations. Outwardly it will resemble an "arabesque," an "artfully ordered confusion" and a "charming symmetry of contradictions"[8] representative of the order of being and the chaos of becoming. It will be "at once completely subjective and individual, and completely objective and like a necessary part in a system of all the sciences" (*A* 77, *KA* 2:176).

Originating in philosophy, ironic art will operate in the "scientific spirit" of "conscious philosophy" (*L* 108, *KA* 2:160). Just as "we wouldn't think much of an uncritical transcendental philosophy that doesn't represent the producer along with the product and contain within the system of transcendental thought a description of transcendental thinking," so the ironic artist will "unite the transcendental raw materials and preliminaries of a theory of poetic creativity . . . with . . . artistic reflection and beautiful self-mirroring" (*A* 238, *KA* 2:204). He not only offers a representation of the universe (*KA* 18:213, frag. 219) but also shows how his representation came to be (*KA* 12:102). With his "clear consciousness of eternal agility, of an infinitely teeming chaos" (*I* 69, *KA* 2:263), the ironic artist attempts to render or evoke the infinite in his creation of a fiction or system. But he questions it as an accurate representation of the chaos of becoming and in the act of doing so soon discovers that it is but a mere construct of his own making, an inadequate and fragmentary exposition of infinite becoming, from which he recoils and which he undermines, in effect de-creating his own creation. The gap between representation and presence resulting from the "indissoluble antagonism between the absolute and the relative" (*L* 108, *KA* 2:160), he indicates by self-representation; which is to say that he makes his art a representation of the act of representation in order to show the limits of the activity and at the same time hold on to the evocation of the infinite manifested in his art. That is why *Universalpoesie* is a "form so fit for expressing the entire spirit of the author" and why "many artists who started to write only a novel ended up by providing us with a portrait of themselves" (*A* 116, *KA* 2:182).

Bearing a somewhat similar relation to his poem as the Christian God does to the cosmos, the poet may be said paradoxically to be both *in* and *out* of the creation, immanent *and* transcendent. Hovering above his work but free to enter it as he pleases, the artist is like the *buffo* in comic opera or the Harlequin figure in *commedia dell'arte,* who at the same time controls the plot and mocks the play, or like the parabasis of Greek drama in which the author's spokesman, usually the chorus, interrupts the action of the play to address the audience on matters of concern to the author. Engaged in constant "self-creation and self-destruction" (*L* 37, *KA* 2:151), the ironist is committed to "continuous self-parody" (*L* 108, *KA* 2:160). Irony is permanent parabasis, Schlegel insisted (*KA* 18:85, frag. 668), parabasis and chorus being necessary to every ironic work "for potentiation."[9] Such a work is "informed by a truly transcendental buffoonery" and in its execution will appropriate "the mimic style of an averagely gifted Italian *buffo*" (*L* 42, *KA* 2:152).

As Anne Mellor points out in her valuable book, the author's making known his presence need not necessarily mean a deliberate destruction of the fictional illusion (pp. 17–18). Often it is accomplished by use of opposing voices or ideas or artistic structures that remain unharmonized. In the sustained and unreconciled opposition of polar points of view the author yields precedence to no particular voice but positions himself above the discourse as a kind of impartial umpire, although he occasionally descends to manifest himself in certain aspects of his creation. As the quotation by Henry Sidgwick cited above indicates, this dialectical irony recognizes that the opposite of what one says may well be true, and thus it never entirely denies an alternative as it hovers between possibilities. It refuses to be forced into a stance of either/or but insists on the posture of both/and.

Yet even in this instance of dialectical irony the fictional illusion is broken by the artist's insistence, sometimes explicit but more often implicit, that his work is not a representation of reality but an *artistic* re-presentation, that it is first and foremost an artifact, pure artifice that aims to "describe itself," being "simultaneously poetry and the poetry of poetry" (*A* 238, *KA* 2:204). Like the artist himself, it transcends itself: "it can . . . hover at the midpoint between the portrayed and the portrayer, free of all real and ideal self-restraint, on the wings of poetic reflection, and can raise that reflection again and again to a higher power, can multiply it in an endless succession of mirrors" (*A* 116, *KA* 2:182). Insofar as it depicts, a work of romantic irony portrays itself.

In this "hovering" (*Schweben*) of artist and artwork itself the element of game and play is present. The ambiguity, mobility, and paradox of ontological becoming that inform art and life alike require an agility, a brisk and nimble stretch characteristic of all kinds of play. "Poetic illusion," says Schlegel, "is a game of impressions, and the game, an illusion of actions" (*A* 100, *KA* 2:180). To shatter this illusion is to introduce another dimension to the game, for it means that the pieces have to be put back together for the game to proceed: "The fact that one can annihilate a philosophy . . . or . . . can prove that a philosophy annihilates itself is of little consequence. If it's really philosophy, then, like the phoenix, it will always rise again from its own ashes" (*A* 103, *KA* 2:180).

Irony, being "involuntary and yet completely deliberate dissimulation" (*L* 108, *KA* 2:160), is play in the theatrical sense as well, in that it requires one to enact roles. The ironic author not only plays the role of stage manager or master of ceremonies but, like Harlequin, also assumes a part in the play. In addition, he at times endows his characters with the consciousness that they too are actors in a literary vehicle, so that while seeming to possess free will, they nevertheless are aware of being puppets controlled by the author or his spokesman in the play; just as in real life human beings are granted the illusion of freedom of choice while at the same time they are hemmed in, and the scope of their choice is narrowed by mountains of necessity. Joyfully embracing the voluntary and necessary dissimulation in both life and art, Schlegel demands "that events, men, in short the play of life, be taken as play and be represented as such" (*DP*, p. 89).

Because indeterminacy or the unsettling of meaning follows from the playful hovering of the author above the text that represents the world of becoming, irony avoids closure. Where other kinds of poetry can be finished and rounded out, all its parts brought together into formal perfection, "the romantic kind of poetry is still in the state of becoming; that, in fact, is its real essence: that it should forever be becoming and never be perfected" (*A* 116, *KA* 2:182); it is "open" (*L* 117, *KA* 2:162). Yet, while recognizing the impossibility of enclosure, some authors may nevertheless seek to achieve something like it by lengthy elaboration, wanting "to say a great many things that absolutely ought to be left unsaid" (*L* 33, *KA* 2:150) and "to blurt out everything" (*L* 37, *KA* 2:151). Such a person has not learned the value of self-restriction. The writer "who can and does talk himself out, who keeps nothing back for himself, and likes to tell everything he knows, is to be pitied" because thereafter there is nothing left for him to say. Given the revolutionary potential of time in a world of becoming, a person can change his mind in a minute and not wish to proceed along the course inspired by his initial enthusiasm: "Even a friendly conversation which cannot be broken off at any moment, completely arbitrarily, has something intolerant about it" (*L* 37, *KA* 2:151). The poetry of becoming, which recognizes both "the impossibility and the necessity of complete communication" (*L* 108, *KA* 2:160), will necessarily be fragmentary.

Throughout his own literary fragments Schlegel is concerned to put a rein on the hovering subject glorifying in its own activity. Where on the one hand he endorses romantic irony's grant of transcendence to the creative subject of its image and representational system, on the other hand he is careful, as Gary Handwerk has brilliantly shown, to indicate that irony is not only aesthetic and metaphysical play but also ethical endeavor. The artist who wants to blurt out everything in self-display "fails to recognize the value and dignity of self-restriction, which is after all, for the artist as well as for the man, the first and the last, the most necessary and the highest duty." It is most necessary, Schlegel says, "because wherever one does not restrict oneself, one is restricted by the world," which is to say that one is unheeded or cast off, "and that makes one a slave." It is the highest duty "because one can only restrict oneself at those points and places where one possesses infinite power, self-creation, and self-destruction" (*L* 37, *KA* 2:151); which is to say that the ironic artist must restrain his tendency to conquer, overcome, and in effect violate his audience by forcing his own will, his own sense of self, on an other.

For Schlegel irony is both egotistically sublime and negatively capable. As power, an unbridled assertion of subjectivity, it is imperialistic, aiming to embrace, order, and absorb everything. As love, it desires a reciprocal relationship with an other. "It contains and arouses a feeling of indissoluble antagonism . . . between the impossibility and the necessity of complete communication" (*L* 108, *KA* 2:160). On the one hand the ironist, contemptuous of conventional representational systems, wishes to tell all and to tell it all at once in a language of his own devising; on the other hand he wishes to share feelings and insights with an other, which means that, recognizing literature to be "republican speech" (*L* 65, *KA* 2:155), he must subdue himself to that which can be represented and communicated. Hence irony is an interplay between self-assertion and self-restraint that allows to "occur in the other person that which took place in us, and the aim of communication [thereby to be] attained" (*KA* 12:102). The notion of communication and dialogue with the reader figures strongly in Schlegel's thoughts on irony. First, it is conceived of as a means of conceptualizing and attaining a sense of selfhood. As Gary Handwerk points out, "Irony is above all a certain way of dealing with the problem of the subject in language and its apparent communicative isolation" (p. 44). Schlegel says that "nobody understands himself who does not understand his fellows. Therefore you first have to believe you are not alone" (*I* 124, *KA* 2:268). Intersubjectivity—the dialogue between subjects, not between subject and object—raises the individual subject to a higher level of consciousness. "To mediate and to be mediated are the whole higher life of man," Schlegel says (*I* 44, *KA* 2:260). No one can live without a "vital center," a sense of self, and if one does not possess it, then one can seek it only in an other, for only an other's "center can stimulate and awaken his own" (*I* 45, *KA* 2:260). No endeavor is so truly human "as one that simply supplements, joins, fosters" (*I* 53, *KA* 2:261). Second, the notion of communication is conceived in a larger, ethical sense, as sympathy becomes a fundamental requisite for art. The artist must aim "to communicate . . . and share . . . with somebody, not simply express himself" (*L* 98, *KA* 2:178). "Real sympathy concerns itself with furthering the freedom of others," not merely with personal satisfaction (*A* 86, *KA* 2:178). As Schlegel pondered the nature of ironic art, he envisioned an increasingly larger role for the reader, to the point where the reader actually becomes engaged in the creation of the work. Unlike the "analytic writer" who wishes only to address the reader and make an impression upon him, the ironic artist, a "synthetic writer," does not imagine the reader to be "calm and dead, but alive and critical." The synthetic writer provides the fragments which the reader must construe and discover the meaning of for himself. Thus the ironic artist does not try to make any particular impression upon the reader "but enters with him into the sacred relationship of deepest symphilosophy or sympoetry" (*L* 112, *KA* 2:161). In brief, the writer enters into "a philosophy of friendship" (*Blütenstaub* 2, *KA* 2:164) by means of "a dialogue [which] is a chain or garland of friendships" (*A* 77, *KA* 2:176). As Schlegel's contemporary, the poet Friedrich von Hardenberg (better known as Novalis) says, "The true reader must be the extended author. He is the higher tribunal, which receives the matter from the lower tribunal already preworked."[10] Schlegel envisioned a still further step when in the future symphilosophy and sympoetry would become so universal and intimate that it would not be unusual if two minds that complement each other were "to create communal works of art" (*A* 125, *KA* 2:185).

This ideal of complementarity, the joining of two minds together "like divided halves that can realize their own full potential only when joined" (*A* 125, *KA* 2:185), enlarges Schlegel's conception of role playing beyond the notion of mere play to an understanding that it involves entering into a closer relationship with an other so as to supplement one's own perspectives. It is in fact seen as another form of dialogue, which intends "to set against one another quite divergent opinions, each of them capable of shedding new light upon [a subject] from an individual standpoint, each of them striving to penetrate from a different angle into the real heart of the matter" (*DP* p. 55). In like fashion, parabasis, said to be necessary to every ironic work "for potentiation" (*LN* frag. 1682), is to be seen not only as the breaking of the fictional illusion but also as an opening up of space for the response of the audience and its inclusion into the making of the work. As Novalis said, "We should transform everything into a

Thou—a second I—only thereby do we raise ourselves to the Great I—which is *one* and *all* simultaneously."[11]

From this survey of German idealist thought on the subject we can see that if romantic irony seems to elude definition, it nevertheless has some defining characteristics. Philosophically it is founded on the gap between being and becoming, which Nietzsche later was to represent as the Apollonian and Dionysian disjuncture. Being is characterized by the Apollonian drive toward order, fixity, individuation, and objectivity; it is by nature temporal, finite, conscious, and masculine. Becoming, on the other hand, is characterized by the Dionysian drive toward chaos, fluidity, subjectivity, and cosmic oneness; partaking of the eternal and the infinite, it is by nature unconscious and feminine. Romantic irony seeks to lessen the gap, to negate the abyss between subject and object, to get at the Absolute Ego behind the finite ego, in full realization, however, that the material world can never be transformed into spirit, that the gap may be narrowed but never closed. In Nietzschean terms romantic irony wears a "Janus face, at once Dionysiac and Apollonian," which may be expressed in the formula "Whatever exists is both just and unjust, and equally justified in both."[12]

A literary work in this mode has many and often all of the following characteristics. Formally it is an arabesque, a mixture of styles, modes, and genres. It avoids closure and determinate meaning as it deconstructs the invented fictional world that it pretends to offer. Essentially reflexive, sometimes to the point of infinite regress, it mirrors its author and itself. Concerned with the question of human freedom, it displays the oppressiveness of being and materiality, designated as fate, frequently by presenting characters who conceive of themselves as dramatis personae. It is distrustful of its own linguistic medium and invites the "sym-poetic" participation of the reader. Permeated by a sense of play, it permits the creative self to hover above its image and representational system and thereby glorify in its own self-activity.

I propose in the following chapters to present Carlyle, Thackeray, Browning, Arnold, Dickens, Tennyson, and Pater as romantic ironists by examining some of their works. Insofar as it has been applied to English authors, romantic irony, as I suggested earlier, has been associated chiefly with the Romantics and hardly at all with the Victorians. I do not claim that all the authors I treat were acquainted with Schlegel or other German philosophers and writers on the subject. Some of them were, and some of them probably were not: Carlyle, Thackeray, Tennyson, Arnold, and Pater were avid readers of the German idealists; Browning seemed somehow to be acquainted with them, although he disclaimed having read them; Dickens had little interest in formal philosophy. The point is irrelevant, however, for as we have seen, by 1830 the notion of change was in the air and among advanced thinkers, the concept of becoming was a dominant idea. It took no philosophical training to arrive at the conclusion that meaning had become problematical and that suspended judgment was therefore desirable. Once the doctrine of becoming, eternal change without telos, was embraced, it followed as the night the day that an ironic, a romantic ironic world view was the result. Moreover, for an author this meant that his way of regarding the world required an artistic mode correspondent to it. Which is to say, Carlyle, Thackeray, Browning, Arnold, Dickens, Tennyson, and Pater became romantic ironists in no small part because the *Zeitgeist* demanded it.

Because their work is what Schlegel called "an image of the age" (*A* 116, *KA* 2:182), their irony is not an eighteenth-century rhetorical irony nor a twentieth-century irony of negative absurdity. To put it another way, Victorian romantic irony is not subsumed by either the normative irony or the epistemological irony espoused by the two chief contemporary theorists of literary irony. Arguing that irony's complexities are shared by the author and the reader, Wayne C. Booth insists that irony is rhetorically functional and that beneath every ironic surface there is a stable center of determinate meaning to be uncovered. Paul de Man, on the other hand, emphasizing the duplicitous nature of language and the consequent breakdown of understanding, holds that the interpretation of an ironic text is impossible because there is no stable center of meaning, "meaning" being an illusion of the conscious mind imprisoned within its own linguistic system but desiring release into metaphysics.[13] In brief, Booth reconstructs, de Man deconstructs, while Victorian romantic irony does both.

For separately reconstructionist and deconstructionist theories of irony obviate possibility—the possibility of becoming. When deconstructionists insist on the death of meaning, they reify a meaning that precludes all others. And when reconstructionists maintain that a statement of meaning can be recovered, they too lapse into dogma and affirm meaning as something fixed and final. Victorian romantic ironists, however, are less concerned with meaning than with the possibility of meaning. Which is to say that for them meaning is neither fixed nor absent; it is always becoming, realizing itself in different styles, forms, modes, and perspectives. For them meaning is provisional, sometimes perhaps nothing more than a fiction but nevertheless an enabling fiction in a world of possibilities.

1

CARLYLE'S *THE FRENCH REVOLUTION*
A "True Fiction"

In part because the term derives from the German word for novel (*Roman*), romantic irony has been associated almost exclusively with works of fiction, mainly the novel, the tale, and the drama.[1] Seldom has it been related to historical narrative. This has meant that in the case of Carlyle, one of the few Victorians recognized as a romantic ironist, critics have dealt with *Sartor Resartus* as a work in this mode but have not seen that *The French Revolution* is equally an example of what Schlegel called progressive universal poetry.[2]

Another reason why critics have not recognized *The French Revolution* as a work of romantic irony is owing to their attempts to fit it into one of the traditional genres. Long before Hayden White's classifications of nineteenth-century written histories according to their emplotments, commentators on *The French Revolution* were concerned to determine its genre. According to some it is an epic, to others a tragedy. The most recent critic of Carlyle as a historian holds that it is "closer in spirit to epic than to tragedy" in that as "heroic narrative" it "embodies the dominant impulse of the literary imagination in any age . . . by which the panoramic and the particular, the cosmic and the local, the mythic and the historic, are held in the most fruitful tension."[3] This generous definition of epic does subsume many aspects of Carlyle's history, but it does not take into account that *The French Revolution* is as much an antiheroic narrative as a heroic one, that it questions the ability of the narrator to relate the story accurately because of the limitations of language, deconstructs the invented historico-poetical world that it claims to offer, demands the complicity of the reader in its telling, evades closure and settled meaning, and constantly calls attention to itself not as history but as linguistic artifact.

I propose that *The French Revolution* is essentially neither an epic nor a tragedy but rather a work of romantic irony in which many genres are mingled. Carlyle did not cease to be a romantic ironist with the completion of *Sartor Resartus,* as has been claimed.[4] For what is characteristic of *Sartor* (composed 1830–31) is, to a great extent, likewise characteristic of *The French Revolution* (written 1834–37); which is to say that Carlyle's way of perceiving the world continued to require an artistic mode correspondent to his world view, namely, a romantic ironic one.

Carlyle's world as presented in *The French Revolution* is ever in motion, "not fixable; not fathomable . . . but for ever growing and changing."[5] Here "there is properly nothing else but revolution and mutation, and even nothing else conceivable" (2:211). Out of the abundant and fertile chaos of becoming, imaged usually as a roiling, ever-turbulent sea or sometimes as a flood of lava, there arise islands of cosmos: "Dim Chaos, or the sea of troubles, is struggling through all its elements; writhing and chafing towards some Creation" (4:157). The creation lasts, however, but for a while, and indeed contains within itself the elements of its dissolution: "The Beginning holds in it the End" (3:103). And then after "dissolutions, precipitations, endless turbulence of attracting and repelling . . . this wild alchemy arrange[s] itself again" (4:116). Chaos becomes cosmos, which in turn becomes chaos, and so on ad infinitum.

Underlying and informing this world of becoming is the infinite, expressing itself throughout time in "Realised Ideals," myths or symbols embodying the highest apprehension of truth at

a given time. "How such Ideals do realise themselves; and grow,
wondrously, from amid the incongruous ever-fluctuating chaos of
the Actual"—this, says Carlyle, "is what World-History . . . has
to teach us. How they grow . . . bloom out mature, supreme; then
quickly . . . fall into decay; sorrowfully dwindle; and crumble
down, or rush down, noisily or noiselessly disappearing" (2:10).
In brief, history should show how the infinite animates the finite.
     But how is it possible for the historian to represent the tur-
bulent process of becoming in which the infinite is, in part, temporarily realized? Certainly not by conventional narrative means.
For, as Carlyle had remarked in the essay "On History" (1830),
"all Narrative is, by its nature, of only one dimension; only trav-
els forward towards one, or towards successive points: Narrative
is *linear,* Action is *solid*" (27:89). Lived history, on the other
hand, is quite different from written history and cannot be explained in terms of linear, cause-and-effect relationships, as histo-
rians since the Enlightenment have sought to do. Each event is the
offspring not of one but of all other prior or contemporaneous
events and, moreover, will in its turn combine with others to give
birth to new ones:

> it is an ever-living, ever-working Chaos of Being, wherein
> shape after shape bodies itself forth from innumerable elements.
> And this Chaos, boundless . . . and . . . unfathomable . . . is
> what the historian will depict . . . by threading it with single
> lines of a few ells in length! For . . . all Action is, by its
> nature, to be figured as extended in breadth and in depth, as
> well as in length. (27:88)

What, in other words, the written history must display is not mere
successiveness but simultaneity; it must be like the world itself.
     Yet language is linear and seems to preclude such an endeav-
or. The space between word and thing is enormous; mimesis is
impossible. Language is phenomenal and thus cannot deal with
the noumenal that underlies and informs the finite. "The first

word we utter we begin to *err,"* Carlyle was fond of quoting from Goethe.[6] The fact remains, however, that language, whatever its deficiency, is the major tool with which man works and realizes himself. *"Words,* the strangest product of our nature, are also the most potent," Carlyle wrote in his journal in 1830. "Speech is human, Silence is divine; yet also brutish and dead; therefore we must learn *both* arts, they are both difficult."[7] Evidently a method would have to be found by which to represent in language the world of becoming where man stands "in the confluence of Infinitudes" (4:42–43).

Another difficulty in writing the kind of history at which Carlyle aimed is the partiality of witnesses and documents. "For indeed it is well said, 'in every object there is inexhaustible meaning; the eye sees in it what the eye brings means of seeing' " (2:5). Every report is circumscribed by the physical and psychological limitations of its reporter: everyone sees from his or her point of view, and no matter how objective a person wishes to be, one cannot speak of other than what one perceives from one's own angle of vision; with the best of intentions one nevertheless remains *parti pris.* How then can a historian achieve simultaneity and inclusiveness if, first, one must work with partial sources and, second, one writes from one's own viewpoint in reporting them? Is it possible to transcend point of view?

In the early 1830s, as Carlyle found himself more and more drawn to the writing of history, these were the chief obstacles that he foresaw to his enterprise. As for subject, he was intrigued by the French Revolution, the most dramatic event within recent times displaying the tempestuous process of becoming and of violent overthrow of "Realised Ideals." To John Stuart Mill he wrote in September 1833: "the right *History* (that impossible thing I mean by History) of the French Revolution were the grand Poem of our Time; . . . the man who *could* write the *truth* of that, were worth all other writers and singers" (*CL* 6:446). The more he thought about undertaking a history of the Revolution, the less capable he felt of achieving what he would like. "Alas, the *thing* I want to do is precisely the thing I cannot do," he told his brother

in October 1833. "My mind would so fain deliver itself ade-
quately of that 'Divine Idea of the World'; . . . one of the subjects that engages me most is the French Revolution, which indeed
for us is still the subject of subjects" (*CL* 7:6). It was, of course,
impossible to represent perfectly the "Divine Idea" at work in
history: such a project "cannot, by the highest talent and effort, be
succeeded in, except in more or less feeble approximation" (*CL*
6:446); "only in quite *in*adequate approximations is such deliverance possible" (*CL* 7:6). Yet, he told Mill, "the attempt *can* be
made" (*CL* 6:446).

As a trial effort Carlyle in 1833 composed "The Diamond
Necklace," "to prove [himself] in the Narrative style" (*CL* 7:7).[8]
Borrowing the romantic ironic techniques employed in *Sartor
Resartus,* he made the work an arabesque of multiple voices,
clashing perspectives, interruptions of the narrative for addresses
to the reader, incongruous details, varying literary genres, and
interlocking narrative frames. Aiming for "a kind of . . . *True
Fiction*" as a means of showing "Reality Ideal" (*CL* 7:245, 61),
he treated this episode of French history as a drama in which the
viewer must allow his "*aesthetic* feeling first have play" before
being taken backstage to satisfy his or her "insatiable scientific
curiosity" (28:360). In effect "The Diamond Necklace" is akin to
the commedia dell'arte, presided over by a comedian who makes
sport of himself, his reader, and his work.

"The Diamond Necklace" was designed to show that if the
historian were to concentrate on an object, "were it the meanest
of the mean," and "paint it in its actual truth . . . an indestructible portion of the miraculous All,—his picture of it were a
Poem"; and, moreover, to show "that Romance exists" and "exists, strictly speaking, in Reality alone" (28:329).[9] The piece was,
said Carlyle, "truly a kind of curiosity" to test whether
"by sticking actually to the Realities of the thing . . . one could
not in a small way make a kind of Poem of it." The result was
"not quite so unsuccessful as one could have expected" (*CL*
7:57).

Pleased with his experiment, Carlyle was now prepared for

action, more or less along the same lines, in a larger theater.[10] To
achieve his drama he realized that he would have to enlist the aid
of his reader. As early as 1828 he had theorized about the role of
the reader, who must be "ever conscious of his own active coöp-
eration" (26:149); and in "The Diamond Necklace" he had insisted on the reader's partnership with the author, the writer supply-
ing what "true historical research would yield" and the reader
bringing "a kindred openness, a kindred spirit of endeavour"
(28:330). In this dynamic, dialogical relationship the meaning is
generated by both the author and the reader, who share in the
moral responsibility of interpreting the fluid text.

From beginning to end of *The French Revolution* the narrator
invites the reader's participation: "Let the Reader . . . endeavour
to look with the mind too" (2:5); "let the Reader fancy" (3:235);
"let the Reader conceive" (4:3); "let the Reader stir up his own
imaginative organ" (4:207). Further, the narrator directs the reader as to how he should act and react: "dull wert thou, O Reader, if
never in any hour . . . it spoke to thee" (2:8–9); "yes, Reader,
that is the Type-Frenchman of this epoch" (2:137); "now, Reader,
thou shalt quit this noisy Discrepancy of a National Assembly"
(2:222); "Reader, fancy not, in thy languid way, that Insurrection
is easy" (3:291). Only through a brotherly relationship between
author and reader is meaning to be apprehended: "therefore let us
two, O Reader, dwell on [this] willingly . . . and from its endless
significance endeavour to extract what may, in present circumstances, be adapted for us" (4:2). Finally, the narrative ends with
the writer's valedictory summation of how the partnership has (or
should have) proceeded:

> And so here, O Reader, has the time come for us two to
> part. Toilsome was our journeying together; not without offence;
> but it is done. To me thou wert as a beloved shade, the
> disembodied or not yet embodied spirit of a Brother. To thee I
> was but as a Voice. Yet was our relation a kind of sacred one;
> doubt not that! For whatsoever once sacred things become

hollow jargons, yet while the Voice of Man speaks with Man,
hast thou not there the living fountain out of which all
sacrednesses sprang, and will yet spring? Man, by the nature of
him, is definable as 'an incarnated Word.' Ill stands it with me
if I have spoken falsely; thine also it was to hear truly.
Farewell. (4:323)

The French Revolution is the closest that Carlyle would ever come
to Schlegel's ideal of synthetist art of symphilosophy and sympoetry, in which the author "constructs and creates his own reader; . . . he makes that which he invented gradually take place
before the reader's eyes, or he tempts him to do the inventing for
himself" (*L* 112, *KA* 2:161).

What the author and reader essentially share is that each is a
linguistic animal, "an incarnated Word." This is both their glory
and their sad destiny. As incarnations they can utter intimations of
the infinite that were otherwise impossible to reveal; yet suffering
the limitations of all embodiments, they cannot speak all that they
would because "human language, unused to deal with these
things, being contrived for the uses of common life," can only
struggle "to shadow out" what it would communicate (4:122).
Like all phenomena, language is subject to decline and decay: it
grows old and is no longer satisfactory as a means of communication. New occasions arise for which there are no adequate words.
When, for example, addressing the final horrors of the Reign of
Terror, "History . . . would try . . . to include under her old
Forms of speech or speculation this new amazing Thing . . . [yet]
in this new stage, History . . . babbles and flounders" (4:203). It
is then that a new language must be forged. This is what, in their
linguistic association, the author and reader together seek. At first
the most they can hope for is a near approach to the right word:
"any approximation to the right Name has value." Thereafter, as
their fraternal union is more fully realized, they hit upon the *mot
juste:* "the Thing is then ours, and can be dealt with" (4:204).
This is not, of course, to say the perfect word can ever be dis-

covered, since the identity of signifier and signified is always proximate at best.

History too has its grammar, and its parts of speech are ever subject to change. As embodied language, humans also can become archaisms unsuited for the grammar of a new or changing era. Thus Louis XV, the representative of absolute monarchy, is, in the final third of the eighteenth century, a "Solecism Incarnate" (2:21). Louis XVI is, in late 1792, "the unhappiest of Human Solecisms" (4:81). They must pass; and so too, in time, with linguistic inevitability, will the aristocrats of the *ancien régime,* for "to such abysmal overturns . . . are human Solecisms all liable" (2:207).

Clearly, a new grammatical combination must arise in the syntactical sentence that is human society. The first effort is to formulate, by legislation, a new grammar. Trying to compose a constitution, the National Assembly "becomes a Sanhedrim of Pedants" debating a *"Theory of Irregular Verbs"* (2:215). As conditions in France worsen, "with Famine and a Constitutional theory of defective verbs going on, all other excitement is conceivable" (3:18). Instead of meaningful language there emerges only the "inarticulate dissonance" of sansculottism. All the while, however, "History, and indeed all human Speech and Reason does . . . strive to *name* the new Things it sees of Nature's producing" although forced to admit "that all Names and Theorems yet known . . . fall short" (4:204). Following the regicide, the Convention becomes "the womb of *Formula,* or perhaps her grave," as the people cry, *"Du pain, pas tant de longs discours"* (4:153, 303). At the end the linguistic outcome is left in doubt: "The new Realities are not yet come; ah no, only Phantasms, Paper models, tentative Prefigurements of such!" (4:322). The last word is given to the "Arch-quack Cagliostro," the appropriate grammarian of the frenzied era, whose "prophecy" in "The Diamond Necklace" has curiously been "fulfilled," or is perhaps "fulfilling" (4:323). In 1795—or in 1837, as the narrator is careful to point out—the new grammar has not yet fully evolved.

One of the ways in which Carlyle attempts to overcome the linearity of the language of narrative is by manipulation of point of view. The narrator usually speaks in the third person, reporting from the overview of the "Eye of History" (2:5 and 3:191, for instance). Not infrequently he interrupts his story for comment, for the length of a chapter (2:52–55), a paragraph (2:6–7), or even part of a sentence (as when he says that no one pays any attention to Besenval, "a thing the man of true worth is used to" [2:130]).[11] Or, assuming the seer's mantle, he speaks with the voice of prophecy:

> What a work, O Earth and Heavens, what a work! Battles and bloodshed, September Massacres, Bridges of Lodi, retreats of Moscow, Waterloos, Peterloos, Tenpound Franchises, Tarbarrels and Guillotines;——and from this present date, if one might prophesy, some two centuries of it still to fight! Two centuries; hardly less; before Democracy go through its due, most baleful, stages of *Quack*ocracy; and a pestilential World be burnt up, and have begun to grow green and young again. (2:133)

In addition to addressing the reader ("Listen," "See," "Note," "Follow"), the narrator occasionally invites him to join in a synoptic view and look from his "coign of vantage . . . with far other eyes than the rest [below] do" (2:135); or he tells the reader what he might see could he reach the tower of Notre Dame (3:291). At times the narrator becomes part of the action by joining the characters of his story:

> And now behold it is vouchsafed us; States-General shall verily be! (2:115)

> Thither will we: King's Procureur [et al.] shall go with us; . . . if he kill us, we shall but die. (2:187)

Or he speaks to the historical figures in the vocative as though he (and the reader) were there:

> Look to it, D'Aiguillon. (2:2)
>
> On then, all Frenchmen, that have hearts in your bodies! (2:190)
>
> If ye dare not, then, in Heaven's name, go to sleep. (3:121)

Sometimes he blends points of view within a single sentence so that he is simultaneously both detached from and involved in the action:

> There also observe Preceptress Genlis, or Sillery, or Sillery-Genlis,—for our husband is both Count and Marquis, and we have more than one title. (3:24)

Finally, the narrator removes himself entirely from the narrative and allows others to tell the story, as when he offers lengthy quotations from various memoirists (4:31–38).

In like manner the narrator constantly shifts tenses, mainly mingling the past with the present but occasionally switching to the future. Though the Revolution occurred over four decades earlier and thus must be largely recounted in the past, the narrator recognizes the falsifications that must necessarily result from doing so. The past tense, he admits, "is a most lying thing," rendering that which is in the distance beautiful and sad, but "one most important element is surreptitiously . . . withdrawn from the Past Time: the haggard element of Fear!" Fear, uncertainty, and anxiety dwell only in the present (4:81), and to suggest these or to induce them within the reader by making him feel he is there at the instant the event took place, the narrator resorts to the historical present indicative. The French Revolution, the narrator says in effect, happened in the past, but even in 1837 it is not yet finished, remaining, to no small degree, a matter of current concern. "Does not, at this hour, a new Polignac . . . sit reflective in the Castle of Ham [and here a footnote reads: 'A.D. 1835']; in an astonishment he will never recover from; the most confused of existing mortals?" (2:224). The son of Philippe Egalité who fought well in Alsatia "is

the same intrepid individual who now, as Louis-Phil-
ippe . . . struggles, under sad circumstances, to be called King of
the French for a season," and who is "frequently shot at, not yet
shot" (4:58, 322). Marat's sister, the narrator says, is still living in
Paris at the very time he is writing of the murder of Marat by
Charlotte Corday (4:170). Sansculottism "still lives . . . still
works . . . till, in some perfected shape, it embrace the whole
circuit of the world!" Its body "need not reappear . . . for another
thousand years. . . . That there be no second Sansculottism . . .
let Rich and Poor of us go and do *otherwise.*—But to our tale"
(4:311–13).

In sum, Carlyle presents this curious juxtaposition of tenses
and points of view in order to involve the reader in the action, to
remind him that it is ongoing, and, at the same time, to caution
him that this is not a presentation of the way things actually were
but only a *history,* a tale, a linguistic representation of the way
they might have been. As the narrator tells us at the beginning, the
world of time is "an unfathomable Somewhat, which is *Not we,*"
that we can only "model" into a history, a construct that "reckons
itself real" (2:6–7). Much will remain unknown about the French
Revolution, as Carlyle recognized from the start, when he noted
that his task was to deal with "the incoherent that would not
cohere" and the "*chaos, which I am to re-create* (*CL* 8:103,209).
The impossibility of ever really knowing what happened is im-
pressed upon us time and again, the narrator constantly telling us
of the paucity of sources and their unreliability: "garralous History, as is too usual, will say nothing where you most wish her to
speak" (3:273); "an unlucky Editor may do his utmost; and after
all require allowances" (4:3). The narrator continually comes before us to say, in effect, that this is not life but art, a tale of some
events that took place almost half a century earlier.

With his many references to the theater, the narrator impresses
upon us that we are witnessing an unfolding drama and will
occasionally be permitted a peek backstage. Paris is "a World's
Amphitheatre" (3:55) in which the audience often "jumps on

Stage" so that what is presented is a "World Topsy-turvied" (3:54). At the trial of the king the court ushers "become as Box-keepers at the Opera" (4:103). In this "world's drama . . . the Mimetic become[s] the Real" (3:18), "theatricality" the actuality (3:236). Even when we are returned from the theater to the world of everyday affairs, the drama continues, which "though not played in any pasteboard Theatre, did . . . enact itself" (3:100). The narrator becomes a stage manager or buffo of commedia dell'arte, who establishes the dramatic illusion only to destroy it and thereby so disorient us that we, like the characters within the history, confuse the world and the stage.

The actors on the stage of history are sentient of their status as dramatis personae. Mirabeau "dies as he has lived: self-conscious, conscious of a world looking on" (3:142). The professional actor Collot d'Herbois carries his talent for "the Thespian boards" over to the stage "of the world's drama" (3:18). Bouillé plays the leading role at Nancy, whereafter the stage manager allows him to "fade into dimness" (3:101). Most of the actors will not, however, merely fade away. They insist upon a grand dramatic exit, a farewell speech or gesture: Madame Roland (4:210), Charlotte Corday (4:148), Danton (4:257), Camille Desmoulins (4:257).

Many of the characters regard themselves as mere puppets. At the Feast of the Supreme Being, Robespierre plays his part as a high priest, assuming the roles of Mahomet and Pontiff; he is fully *"conscious"* of his acting "and *knows* that he is machinery" (4:267). Desmoulins feels himself engaged in "one huge Preternatural Puppet-play of Plots" with someone else "pulling the wires": "Almost I conjecture that I, Camille myself, am a Plot, and wooden with wires." Whereupon the narrator–stage manager remarks, "The force of insight could not further go" (4:156). At the end of its performance each puppet is aware that "what part *it* had to play in the History of Civilization is played," and the buffo–stage manager directs: *"plaudite; exeat!"* (2:231). This self-consciousness on the part of the dramatis personae means they become ironic observers and, to the extent that they doubt the meaningfulness of their actions in the drama, victims of irony as well.

The question of fate and free will and the ironies it involves are continually set before us. The narrator says forthrightly, "Our whole Universe is but an infinite Complex of Forces . . . man's Freedom environed with Necessity of Nature" (3:102). Every man's life is "made up 'of Fate and of one's own Deservings,'" of *Schicksal und eigene Schuld*" (3:147). At every hand the "poor human Will struggles to assert itself," only to discover "endless Necessity environing Freewill" (4:199, 122). This is why the characters view themselves as both free agents and puppets and see the vehicles in which they act as both tragedy and comedy.

As he follows the course of the Revolution, the narrator describes the action as a mixture of literary modes and genres. "Transcendent things of all sorts," he says, "are huddled together; the ludicrous, nay the ridiculous, with the horrible" (2:282). The life of Mirabeau "if not Epic for us, is Tragic" (3:147). The ending of the Terror is the "fifth-act, of this natural Greek Drama, with its natural unities" (4:283). The return of the royal family from Varennes is "comico-tragic," the "miserablest *flebile ludibrium* of a Pickleherring Tragedy" (3:187). An incident occurring at the Fatherland's Altar is "of the Nature of Farce-Tragedy" (3:191), while the Feast of the Supreme Being is presented as pure farce (4:267). The host of women marching to Versailles is "ludicro-terrific" (2:253), and during the Terror "the sublime, the ludicrous, the horrible succeed one another; or rather, in crowding tumult, accompany one another" (4:206–7). Events are described as "Epic transactions" (3:157), although taking place in an unheroic age (2:251). They are related by one who can only "speak, having unhappily no voice for singing" (2:212), for indeed "all Delineation, in these ages, were it never so Epic," consists of "'speaking itself and singing itself'" (4:31). Elements of the burlesque and mock epic abound, as in the flight to Varennes and the narrator's constant use of epithets like "the

Sea-green," referring to Robespierre, and "the People's Friend," referring to Marat. [12] In effect, the allusions to literary modes and genres remind us that we are seeing the "history" of the French Revolution as a *literary* event, a "True Fiction" of "a most fictile world" inhabited by "the most fingent plastic of creatures" (2:6). [13]

For the reader-viewer of *The French Revolution* as well as for the actors in the narrative-drama everything seems to be going on at the same time in the wildest kind of hurly-burly; what the narrator-stage manager calls "this Sahara-waltz of the French Twenty-five millions" (4:4). Frivolity and triviality are almost everywhere intermixed with seriousness. Though in great danger, the royal family cannot decide whether to flee:

> Royalty has always that sure trump-card in its hand: Flight out
> of Paris. Which sure trump-card Royalty . . . keeps ever and
> anon clutching at, grasping; and swashes it forth tentatively; yet
> never tables it, still puts it back again. . . . Royalty . . . will
> not play its trump-card till the honours, one after one, be
> mainly lost; and such trumping of it prove to be the sudden
> finish of the game! (3:136)

To many of the inhabitants of Paris the executions in the city square are splendid public theater, amusements for the bored and distractions for the hungry: "Such a game is playing in this Paris Pandemonium" (3:288). While the guillotine is taking its heaviest toll, "the nightly Theatres are Twenty-three; and the *Salons de danse* are Sixty" (4:245). While "right-arms here grew heavy with slaying, right-arms there were twiddledeeing on melodious catgut" (4:38). The action is choreographed as a kind of *danse macabre*.

Just as literary modes and genres are mixed to give the impression of solid inclusiveness, so the syntax of the narrative is jumbled to jolt the reader out of his customary linear way of reading. When J. S. Mill complained that "what is said in an

abrupt, exclamatory, & interjectional manner were [better] said in
the ordinary grammatical mode of nominative & verb," Carlyle
replied that "the common English mode of writing has to do
with . . . *hearsays* of things; and the great business for me, in
which alone I feel any comfort, is recording the *presence*, bodily
concrete coloured presence of things;—for which the Nomi-
native-and-verb, as I find it Here and Now, refuses to stand me in
due stead" (*CL* 9:15). That is why we find in *The French Revolution* passages such as this, a typical one selected at random:

> Night unexampled in the Clermontais; shortest of the year;
> remarkablest of the century: Night deserving to be named of
> Spurs! Cornet Remy, and those Few he dashed off with, has
> missed his road; is galloping for hours towards Verdun; then,
> for hours, across hedged country, through roused hamlets,
> towards Varennes. Unlucky Cornet Remy; unluckier Colonel
> Damas, with whom there ride desperate only some loyal Two!
> More ride not of that Clermont Escort: of other Escorts, in other
> Villages, not even Two may ride; but only all curvet and
> prance,—impeded by storm-bell and your Village illuminating
> itself. (3:177–78)

The distorted syntax in this lyrical-descriptive passage has the
effect of distracted movement in a pastoral landscape, gallant
aims translated into maladroit action. Carlyle intends not merely
to tell us what a thing is but what it feels like in its "bodily
concrete coloured presence." His style helps make *The French
Revolution* what Carlyle himself called it: "a wild savage Book,
itself a kind of French Revolution" (*CL* 9:116).

As Carlyle *in propria persona* and the narrator say over and
again, all action is one and continuous, to be figured in depth and
breadth as well as in length. Things have no real beginnings, no
sole causes of which they are the result and effect; and in like
fashion they have no real endings: "Homer's Epos . . . does not
conclude, but merely ceases. Such, indeed, is the Epos of Univer-

sal History itself" (4:321). Yet in the practical world one must
start and stop somewhere, even if the ascribed beginning or ending is merely arbitrary, a fictional *terminus a quo* and *terminus ad
quem:* "For Arrangement is indispensable to man" (4:288). One
must be "at once determinate (*bestimmt*) and open."[14] Conveniently, then, Carlyle begins his story with Louis XV in 1744,
when the monarchy was still to some degree a viable "Realised
Ideal." He conveniently closes it with Napoleon and the Directo-
ry, the Revolution not ended but merely displaced, "blown into
space" by Napoleon's whiff of grapeshot (4:320). "Be there method, be there order, cry all men; were it that of the Drill-sergeant!"
(4:288). Or, we might add, were it that of the buffo-narrator.

Ultimately Carlyle's notion of being "at once determinate . . . and open" allowed him to view the French Revolution
with double vision. In the ironic world of becoming, where an
entity is both itself and in the process of transformation to something else—where *a* is both *a* and not *a* but *a becoming b*—*a* can
be prized as a momentary island of cosmos amidst the infinite sea,
a type of "Realised Ideal"; but its metamorphosis into *b* is also to
be valued when its vitality is exhausted.

> Great truly is the Actual; is the Thing that has rescued itself
> from bottomless deeps of theory and possibility, and stands
> there as a definite indisputable Fact, whereby men do work and
> live. . . . Wisely shall men cleave to that, while it will endure;
> and quit it with regret, when it gives way under them. . . .
> [When the Thing] is shattered, swallowed up; instead of a green
> flowery world, there is a waste wild-weltering chaos;—which
> has again, with tumult and struggle, to *make* itself into a world.
> (2:37–38)

We must therefore perceive this world of change, where "Innova-
tion and Conservation wage their perpetual conflict," with double
vision: with sadness for the loss of that which was once tri-
umphant in its claim upon man's moral nature and with hope for

the eventual new "ideal" which dissolution of the old portends. So, says the narrator, "in this world of ours, which has both an indestructible hope in the Future, and an indestructible tendency to persevere as in the Past," we must honor the process of change, the flux of history—not only *a* but also *a becoming b*—which "lures us forward by cheerful promises [of] . . . an Era of Hope" (2:39). This is why Carlyle is never, as many commentators believe him to be, totally condemnatory of the Revolution.[15] From his overview of the events of 1789–95 his narrator sees that it was a necessary evil that offered promise of a future good, now "working imprisoned" but "working towards deliverance and triumph" (2:10). "To hate this poor National Convention is easy," he says of its workings in the autumn of 1792; "to praise and love it has not been found impossible." Here and throughout it is not a question of either/or but of both/and, as the narrator "stand[s] with unwavering eyes, looking" before and after and sympathizing equally with both (4:71).[16]

It is clear that neither epic nor tragedy, nor any one of the traditional genres, could encompass Carlyle's view of the French Revolution. Indeed, all conventional forms and genres would have been restrictions and obstructions. What Carlyle hit upon as the means of reproducing the infiniteness of life and mirroring the eternal process of becoming was the "genre" that he described as "True Fiction" and that Schlegel, in defining his special kind of irony, called universal poetry—a "genre" that "is the only one which is more than a genre, and which is, as it were, poetry itself" (*A* 116, *KA* 2:182). Carlyle had wished to make his "right *History*" of the Revolution "the grand Poem of our Time" (*CL* 6:446). According to Mill, who in his review found it "replete with every kind of interest, epic, tragic, elegiac, even comic and farcical" (p. 23), he achieved just that.

2

VANITY FAIR
Transcendental Buffoonery

Unlike Carlyle's, Thackeray's interest in the process of becoming lies less in its manifestations in cataclysmic, revolutionary events than in its movements in society and in social classes. In his works time creates and time destroys, but it is never explosive. Even where momentous episodes of history occur in his fictions, they are always in the background, serving as backdrops in front of which more local incidents of change take place. As the narrator in *Pendennis* observes, "When we talk of this man or that woman being no longer the same person . . . and remark changes [in him or her], we don't . . . calculate that circumstance only brings out the latent defect or quality, and does not create it. . . . [O]ur mental changes are like our grey hairs or our wrinkles—but the fulfilment of the plan of mortal growth and decay."[1] As "a Whig & a Quietist,"[2] Thackeray believed that the big historical moments are essentially like the smaller ones, incidents in the process of becoming. The world is the same everywhere, whether it be England in the time of the later Stuarts (as in *Henry Esmond*) or America at the time of the Revolution (as in *The Virginians*). *Plus ça change, plus c'est la même chose:* this is the basic irony of Thackeray's novels, which, in their delineation of social mobility, offer themselves as fiction that is true.

Perhaps nowhere is Thackeray's concern with the irony of

34

change more evident than in *Vanity Fair,* his second novel but the first to touch on a historical event of outstanding importance. Apparently his early conception of the book was that it would deal with the Battle of Waterloo. In 1842 during a visit in Ireland to Charles Lever, whose novel *Charles O'Malley* (1839) had centered on that battle, the author discussed Waterloo with two experts on the subject. He listened to their explanations of the armies' manoeuvres but concluded that he would "never understand the least about such matters." Although he wished to write on the subject himself, he then "did not see his way clearly," for he was "much inclined to 'laugh at martial might' " while also holding "to the idea that 'something might be made of Waterloo.' "[3] This report of his remarks provides a clue to Thackeray's attitude toward his novel: from the beginning he would approach his material in a serious as well as humorous fashion, from the standpoint of one who is both interested and disinterested in the action.

In the finished novel there is evidence everywhere of this admixture, not least (as in the case of *The French Revolution*) in the narrator's consideration of the literary genre of his work. When it appeared in serial parts (1847–48), *Vanity Fair* bore on its title page the subtitle "Pen and Pencil Sketches of English Society"; when published as a book (1848), it was subtitled "A Novel without a Hero." Within the work itself it is more frequently referred to as a history (pp. 80, 151, 454, 641), "of which every word is true" (p. 602), composed by one calling himself a historian (p. 553) and a chronicler (p. 217).[4] But it is also termed a "Comic History" (p. 475), "a homely story" (p. 55), a "mere story-book" (p. 180), a "tale" (p. 504), a "genteel and sentimental novel" (p. 130), and a "play" (p. 666). In addition it contains many passages of burlesque and parody of contemporary writers, employs epic epithets in a comic manner, and subtly suggests that the story to be expounded is of epic nature.[5] In sum, the work confesses itself to be what Schlegel insisted was the essential form of a work of romantic irony, namely, an arabesque, a generic potpourri.[6]

Presiding over this variegated mixture is a narrator whose roles are diverse and whose dress is that of a clown. Shown on the title pages of the serial issues and the book is the buffo, called in the prologue ("Before the Curtain") "the Manager of the Performance" (p. 5). He introduces the "Puppets" in "the Show" to follow, then "retires, and the curtain rises" (p. 6). But who is this "Manager" dressed in motley and, on the title page of the book, looking into a cracked mirror in which we can see a face reflected? Apparently he is partially to be identified with the author himself, because Thackeray in one of his illustrations depicts himself holding an actor's mask and a jester's wand (p. 87) and says, a few pages earlier, that the figure "holding forth on the cover" is "an accurate picture of your humble servant" (p. 80). This partial congruence is discernible in the prologue, where the actor both is and is not the stage manager. There we are told, in the third person, about the manager and the scene he looks on and then, in a switch to the first person, about the moral, the scenes, the scenery, and the illumination by "the Author's own candles" (that is, his illustrations). A few more words are uttered, seemingly in propria persona, followed by a brief final paragraph in which it is related how the manager bows to his audience and retires as the curtain rises.

This partial identity of the author with the Manager of the Performance in the prologue suggests the manner in which *Vanity Fair* is narrated.[7] For after the curtain rises, the narrator appears in two roles: as a detached, seemingly objective, third-person omniscient narrator looking down on his creation and commenting upon its characters and events and, at the same time, as a character in his work who suffers the same limitations of knowledge as the other actors. Thus while we find him proclaiming himself "the novelist, who knows everything" (pp. 318, 351), we also see him admitting to ignorance: "I don't know in the least" (p. 35); "I think" (p. 80); "My belief is" (p. 150); "It seems to me" (p. 151); "I wonder" (p. 188); "I hope it was" (p. 591). Indeed, on certain occasions he claims to have information about various matters only because it was provided by other characters in the fiction:

> as Captain Dobbin has since informed me (p. 207)
> I was told by Dr. Pestler (p. 377)
> it was only through Mrs. Bute . . . that the circum-
> stances . . . were ever known (p. 386)
> Tom Eaves . . . knew all the great folks . . . and the
> stories and mysteries of each [and told the narrator about Gaunt
> House] (p. 453)
> Tapeworm . . . poured out . . . such a history about Becky
> and her husband . . . and supplied all the points of this
> narrative (p. 644).

Further, he apologizes for his inability to render certain scenes accurately because of his linguistic inadequacy:

> as no pen can depict (p. 16)
> If I had the pen of a Napier, or a Bell's life, I should like
> to describe this combat properly (p. 49)
> Who can tell the dread with which that catalogue was
> opened and read! (p. 340)
> it does not become such a feeble and inexperienced pen as
> mine to attempt to relate (p. 463).

Lastly, the narrator cannot make up his mind whether this book subtitled "A Novel without a Hero" does or does not have any heroic characters. Early on he alludes to "the heroine of this work, Miss Sedley" (pp. 19–20), yet at the end he calls Amelia "our simpleton" and "a tender little parasite" (pp. 637, 661). Then he decides, "If this is a novel without a hero, at least let us lay claim to a heroine [Becky]" (p. 288), whereupon he is concerned to show her up as anything but heroic. He calls Dobbin, who is morally the most attractive person in the book and thus worthy of the sobriquet "rugged old oak" (p. 661), "a spooney"

(p. 641). Yet in a footnote in the first edition the author refers to "my heroes and heroines" (p. 65).[8]

The author enjoys the Godlike ability to be both immanent and transcendent, both in and out of his creation. Not infrequently he even portrays himself as one of the dramatis personae:

> The other day I saw Miss Trotter (p. 113)
> I have heard Amelia say (p. 163)
> I saw Peggy with the infantine procession (p. 218)
> It was on this very tour [of the Rhine] that I . . . had the pleasure to see them [Dobbin and Amelia] first, and to make their acquaintance (p. 602).

This is the character who is "the writer of these pages" (p. 73), "an observer of human nature" (p. 152), "moi qui vous parle" (p. 484), "the present writer . . . [who] was predestined . . . to write [Amelia's] memoirs" (p. 603). Most often he is portrayed (or portrays himself) as a painstaking historian who verifies the accuracy of his narrative ("the present writer went to survey with eagle glance the field of Waterloo" [p. 261]), as a moralist ("Here is an opportunity for moralising!" [p. 140]), and as a keen "observer of human nature" (p. 152). Yet this particularized "I" can upon occasion become the generalized "'I' . . . here introduced to personify the world in general" (p. 350).

This confusion about the proper identity of the "I" is reflected in the narrative process, which is chiefly characterized by frequent interruptions of the story that serve to break the fictional illusion. First, the narrator never lets us forget that he is indeed the Manager of the Performance and manipulator of the characters and the situations in which they are engaged. In certain scenes, he says, "I intend to throw a veil" (p. 66), "bring our characters forward" (p. 81), "adroitly shut the door" (p. 571), and "dwell upon this period" (p. 601). He mounts the stage "to introduce [his characters]" and then "step[s] down from the platform [to] talk about them" (p. 81). He explains why some incidents are included or omitted: "We are not going to write the history [of Mr. Sedley's last years]; it would be too dreary and stupid" (p. 549). He comments on the composition and arrangement of his work: "Although all the little incidents must be heard, yet they must be put off when the great events make their appearance, . . . and hence a little trifling disarrangement and disorder was excusable and becoming" (p. 236); "here it is—the summit, the end—the last page of the third volume" (p. 661) (which in fact it is not).

Second, the narrator intrudes material of marginal relevance into his narrative. He recollects events of the past: "I know . . . an old gentleman of sixty-eight, who said to me one morning at breakfast" (p. 18); "the writer . . . cannot but think of it with a sweet and tender regret" (p. 73); "I remember one night being in the Fair myself" (p. 148); "I . . . look back with love and awe to that Great Character in history" (p. 459). He apostrophizes his characters: "You [Amelia], too, kindly, homely flower!" (p. 167); "My dear Miss Bullock, I do not think *your* heart would break in this way" (p. 171); "Ah! Miss Ann, did it not strike you . . . ?" (p. 581); "Goodbye, Colonel—God bless you, honest William!—Farewell dear Amelia" (p. 661). He apostrophizes a friend: "Do you remember, dear M——, oh friend of my youth . . . ?" (p. 459). He addresses "ladies" (p. 48) and "young ladies" (pp. 172, 652) on matters of taste and decorum and, as we shall presently see, he constantly speaks to the reader.

Third, while commenting at length on the morality of Vanity Fair, the narrator anticipates and attempts to ward off disparaging comments that might be made about the work at hand:

> [Certain] details, I have no doubt, JONES, who reads this book at his Club, will pronounce to be excessively foolish, trivial, twaddling, and ultrasentimental. Yes; I can see Jones at this minute . . . , taking out his pencil. . . . Well, he is a lofty man of genius, and admires the great and heroic in life and novels; and so had better take warning and go elsewhere. (p. 15)

In a footnote in the first edition the narrator vouches for his accuracy: "If anybody considers this an overdrawn picture . . . I refer them to contemporaneous histories" (p. 106). He refuses to include certain matter because of the offense it might offer to his readers' sensibilities, speaking of incidents "hardly fit to be explained" (p. 130) and so "pass[ed] over . . . with that lightness and delicacy which the world demands" (p. 617), of language "which it would do no good to repeat in this place" (p. 158), and of curses which "no compositor in Messrs. Bradbury and Evans's [Thackeray's publishers'] establishment would venture to print . . . were they written down" (p. 273).

Adding to the curious mixture of the fictional and the real is the narrator's treatment of history. The story takes place over the period 1813–30, and Thackeray was at pains to depict as accurately as possible the historical events and period coloring. He has his fictional characters encountering historical personages under perfectly credible circumstances—for example, Lord Steyne and Philippe Egalité (p. 452), Becky and King George IV (p. 459). Almost no detail is amiss in the historical framework: in the Waterloo episode we can easily believe that "Napoleon is flinging his last stake, and poor little Emmy Sedley's happiness forms, somehow, part of it" (p. 167). Yet having taken such effort with the historical details, Thackeray then presents the most jarring anachronisms, which serve in effect to undo the historical picture so carefully constructed. Here are some examples:

> It was the last charge of the Guard—(that is, *it would* have been, only Waterloo had not yet taken place) (p. 49)
> Had orange blossoms been invented then . . . , Miss Maria . . . would have assumed the spotless wreath (p. 113)
> Varnished boots were not invented as yet (p. 207).

Further, the narrator adds comments on how Apsley House and St. George's Hospital look different at the present time from the way they were in 1815, on how the Pimlico triumphal arch and "the

hideous equestrian monster which pervades it and the neigh-
bourhood" did not exist then (p. 206). Finally, in his drawings—
the "Pencil Sketches" of the subtitle of the serial publication—
Thackeray did not represent his characters in the fashions of the
early nineteenth century but in those of his own time. In a note he
explained:

> It was the author's intention, faithful to history, to depict
> all the characters of this tale in their proper costumes, as they
> wore them at the commencement of the century. But when I
> remember the appearance of people in those days, . . . I have
> not the heart to disfigure my heroes and heroines by costumes
> so hideous; and have, on the contrary, engaged a model of rank
> dressed according to the present fashion. (p. 65)

Real and unreal, fact and fiction—the intermixture almost
induces vertigo. What appears at first to be a representation of fact
turns out to be but a reflection of a reflection, an infinite regress of
distance from the thing itself, as on a box of Quaker Oats. The
narrator even seems to allude to the operation of this mirroring
effect: "The great glass over the mantel-piece, faced by the other
great consol glass at the opposite end of the room, increased and
multiplied between them the brown Holland bag in which the
chandelier hung; until you saw these brown Holland bags fading
away in endless perspectives, and this apartment . . . seemed the
centre of a system of drawing-rooms" (pp. 414–15). The center
only *seems*, the fact turns out to be an illusion. Here the narrative
approaches the pure negativity that de Man sees as characteristic
of all irony. But almost immediately the buffo narrator assumes an
existential posture and returns to the world of meaning as he
reverts to his role of moralist, saying that it is just as well that the
actors in such a world rarely see matters for what they are: for is a
person "much happier when he sees and owns his delusion?" (p.
421).

The sense of mimesis, of acting roles, of not being fully in control of their actions is shared by most of the characters.[9] Vanity Fair is after all inhabited, as the Manager of the Performance tells us, by "actors and buffoons" engaged in their "performances" (p. 5), in charades and other "little dramas" (p. 492). Becky is "a perfect performer" (p. 66), with a wide repertory of both speaking and singing parts (p. 659). She can, for example, act "in a most tragical way" (pp. 143–44) or can assume "the part of a Maintenon or a Pompadour" (p. 463). She is, says Lord Steyne, "a splendid actress and manager" (p. 506). Amelia, after her husband's death, plays the role of "the poor widow" (p. 406) who acts "like a tragedy Queen" (p. 448), while her son, much given to acting, "liked to play the part of master" (p. 547). Jane Osborne is "content to be an Old Maid" (p. 416), just as Dobbin, a devoted playgoer, accepts the role of Faithful Unrequited Lover. Miss Horrocks "rehearsed the exalted part" of Lady Crawley, and Sir Pitt "swore it was as good as a play to see her in the character of a fine dame" (p. 389). In one role Lady Southdown was "as magnificent as Mrs. Siddons in Lady Macbeth" (p. 397), while Lady Steyne constantly assumed "tragedy airs" (p. 469). Although the younger Pitt Crawley disapproved of some of Becky's roles and "reprobated in strong terms the habit of play-acting" (pp. 508–9), he is not, in fact, averse to acting roles in which he "had got every word . . . by heart" (p. 398). The narrator continually reminds us that we are witnessing scenes, tableaux, and acts (for example, pp. 66, 143) in "the drama" of *Vanity Fair*.

Acting is tiring, and from time to time the actors express a desire to leave the stage. "I have spent enough of my life at this play," says Dobbin to Amelia, thinking to bid farewell to his role of Loyal Suitor (p. 648). "O brother wearers of motley," asks the narrator, "Are there not moments when one grows sick of grinning and tumbling, and the jingling of cap and bells?" (p. 180). The answer is of course yes, but for the actors in Vanity Fair, no matter how much they may think otherwise, there is no alternative. For they are victims of fate—or of the drama, as it were. As the Manager of the Performance says, they are puppets offering a "singular performance" (p. 6). The "famous little Becky Puppet," "the Amelia Doll," "the Dobbin Figure," "the richly-dressed figure of the Wicked Nobleman" (p. 6)—all are at the mercy of the author-manager: their life is in him, and when he chooses, they must inevitably retire from the stage. "Come children," he says at the end, apparently to his readers who have witnessed the drama, "let us shut up the box and the puppets, for our play is played out" (p. 666). As the buffo of commedia dell'arte says, "La commedia é finita."

The final words of *Vanity Fair* signal, to some extent, the role of the reader in the work. Throughout, the reader is addressed in various ways: as "kind reader" (p. 373), "beloved reader" (pp. 108, 189, 484), "respected reader" (pp. 222, 350), "dear reader" (p. 373), "astonished reader" (p. 418), "ingenious reader" (p. 553), and "dear and civilised reader" (p. 601). Most tellingly, however, he is apostrophized, in the manner Carlyle addresses him in *The French Revolution,* as "brother" (pp. 81, 180, 251, 374, 454, 585, 586), as one who is asked to join in the creation of the drama. Of him the narrator will "ask leave, as a man and a brother" (p. 81), to present his characters and begin the play. And as "brother wearers of motley" (p. 180) readers will be called upon to "picture" the scene (p. 131) and to "suppose" time to have passed (p. 347), distances to have been travelled (p. 372), characters to feel in a particular way (p. 437). "My friend in motley," the narrator says, "your comedy and mine" (p. 585) are not at all unlike, and this commedia of *Vanity Fair* is a joint endeavor based on similar interests and situations. Thus "you and I . . . are never tired of hearing and recounting the history of that famous action [Waterloo]" (p. 314). "You and I, my dear reader," have "our friends" in common (p. 373). As visitors to the fair we see "our friends the Crawleys," "her ladyship, our old acquaintance," or "Miss Briggs, our old friend" (pp. 426, 418, 400). Grandees are not among our mutual acquaintances, and hence into their portals "the beloved reader and writer hereof may hope in vain to enter," although they can console themselves "by thinking comfortably how miserable our betters may be" (pp. 484, 454). Yet both may imagine what occurs within the great mansions of London, and describing the Gaunt House dinner that Becky attended, the narrator, in a generous gesture of sympoetry, even allows the reader "the liberty of ordering [the dinner] himself so as to suit his fancy" (p. 474).

The liberty of ordering is also granted to the reader at the end of the book, as he is left free to invent the subsequent action.[10] For the puppets are shut up in the box for only a time. There is no reason why the novel ends as it does other than it had to end somewhere. In the fifteenth number (chap. 52) Thackeray was evidently already mindful of the difficulties of closure, for he has his narrator say: "Our business does not lie with the second generation [of Crawleys] . . . , otherwise the present tale might be carried to any indefinite length" (p. 504). What he decided was "to leave everybody dissatisfied and unhappy at the end of the story—we ought all to be with our own and all other stories" (Ray, *Letters* 2:423). There is no death or wedding at the end, such as characterized the popular fiction of the time.[11] Rather there is Becky, who "chiefly hangs about Bath and Cheltenham," never seeing her son or former friends (who avoid her when they accidentally meet); and Dobbin and Amelia thoroughly domesticated, he still writing his "History of the Punjaub." So much for the surface, beyond which we are told nothing. "Which of us is happy in this world?" asks the narrator in the last paragraph. "Which of us has his desire? or, having it, is satisfied?" There is no answer, only the decision to shut the puppet box, "for our play is played out."[12]

The sense of play in *Vanity Fair*—of the author's amusing himself with his characters, their actions, and, to a certain extent, his readers—is pervasive.[13] It is not only for his personal entertainment that Thackeray dangles his puppets before us and thwarts our expectations of what a novel should be. For all his foolery, he nevertheless has a moral design, not a vulgar one of telling us what and what not to approve or condemn but a more subtle one that invites us to see that moral judgment is not always easy.[14] He reminds us that he and we alike are not only visitors to but also participants in the fair, the *Vanitas Vanitatum* (p. 666), subject to all its many distractions, foibles, and sins. Here, says the narrator, *"moi qui vous parle,"* you and I, dear reader, are "brothers," not only to each other but to all the other fairgoers as well.

Thackeray is, however, unwilling to let us leave the fair so readily, with a sermon for farewell. He knows that literature is not life, and he wants us to have a like awareness. By constantly breaking the fictional illusion in order to address his audience, he deprives us of the comfort to be derived solely from reading for the plot. He wants us, as he asks of a reader of another of his novels, to "take the trouble to look under the stream of the story" (Ray, *Letters* 2:457). In fiction, he effectively suggests, it is easy for the reader to make judgments, especially if, as is usually the case, he is guided by the author to certain conclusions. In life, however, such determinations are more problematical, because we can never have in our possession all or, frequently, even an adequate number of facts to make considered judgments possible. To prove his point the author calls upon us to decide certain matters. For example, did Becky kill Jos Osborne? Did she commit adultery with Lord Steyne? What did old Osborne want to say before he died? "But who can tell you the real truth of the matter?" (p. 24). "What *had* happened?" (p. 517). "Was she guilty or not?" (p. 538). Questions such as these are scattered throughout the text. We are not told the answers, and consequently we shall never be sure what they are; at best we can have only a kind of moral intuition about them.

We are not provided with answers because, it turns out, the author, for all his vaunted omniscience, does not have them. When asked whether Becky did indeed kill Jos Sedley, Thackeray himself said, "I don't know!"[15] In quest of the truth about the events in the story his narrator goes to extraordinary lengths. He interrogates Miss Pinkerton's servants about incidents at the school, talks with Dobbin about George and Amelia's wedding, asks Dr. Pestler about Amelia's rearing of her son, discusses with Tom Eaves what went on in the Steyne household. Further, the narrator examines various documents in order to render accurate "this veracious history" (p. 455). He consults the East India Register about Jos's career in India, looks into Road Books describing Lord Steyne's country homes, examines closely the map of Pumpernickel, reads through old newspapers for accounts of battles and parties and for biographical information. Yet from none of these can he gain reliable evidence.

When near the end of his "history" the narrator reveals that he is but repeating an old scandal told to him by Tapeworm, we discover that we have no warrant at all, certainly not from the author, that any of the story is true. Like the narrator we can only "suspect" and "doubt" and join him in saying, as the author said in real life, "I don't know" (p. 35). It is not so much that the narrator has tricked us but that his claim "to know everything" is like that of the gossips Tom Eaves, Wenham, and Lord Tapeworm, who also claim to know everything: it is inferential, largely dependent upon hearsay and fragmentary documentary information.[16] The "historian's" early claim to omniscience is, finally, shown to be baseless.

For, the narrator implies, in the world of lies that is Vanity Fair how can we believe anything?[17] Language, both oral and written, is not to be trusted. As Carlyle discovered when writing his history, what a speaker reveals about a certain situation is but an account from his or her own angle of vision. And egoists that we humans are—whether Becky, Amelia, or any of the other actors at the fair—we see what we want to see and put into words that which shows us to best advantage in our quest for social mobility. "The world," the narrator says, "is a looking-glass, and gives back to every man the reflection of his own face" (p. 19). Words, our only means of access to "history" and "truth," must therefore always remain highly suspect. Thackeray would have us see that any linguistic report, whatever its claim to objective truth, is simply a perspective, often "dictated by interested malevolence" (p. 619).

When we have finished the novel, the illustration on the title page takes on a meaning unforeseen in the beginning and becomes for us the "illumination" Thackeray speaks of in the prologue. The cracked looking glass in the hand of the Manager of the Performance shows, we now understand, a shattered image of self, a fragmented and discontinuous self. What the author, who had presented himself as, inter alia, omniscient narrator, puppeteer, historian, and moralist—what the author sees in his work is, in the last analysis, himself. It is a mirror held up not to nature but to himself and his "brother," the reader, "mon semblable, mon frère."

Unlike Bunyan's pilgrim, who passes through Vanity Fair on a straight road and looks neither to the left nor right, Thackeray's characters are hemmed in by the confines of the fair itself. Like Christian, they strive; but unlike him they seek for what is not worth having, as in their walk around the fair they take the sham for truth. And having achieved the status they sought, they find they are basically unaltered; only the circumstances have changed, and they themselves are subject to "the plan of mortal growth and decay" spoken of in *Pendennis*. As the narrator, in his role as transcendental buffoon, asks in the final paragraph, who has his desire or having it is satisfied? It was the genius of Thackeray to dramatize the irony of becoming in very Victorian terms—by showing us Vanity Fair as the theater of social mobility, replete with both meaning and meaninglessness.

3

LEVITY'S RAINBOW
The Way of Browning's "Christmas-Eve"

The chief question posed by Robert Browning's poetry is that of adequacy: what will suffice? Behind this question lies the metaphor of growth, development, metamorphosis—*Bildung*—that is at the heart of the poet's thinking. Conceiving of the universe in Heraclitean terms of energy, motion, and change, Browning believed that for the individual and for humanity as a whole becoming is the perennial process of development whereby, first, contradictions are felt to be momentarily resolved and the limitations of an outmoded form of consciousness temporarily overcome, and, secondly, this stage is perceived as deficient, so that, thirdly, a new stage of consciousness is attained. Never amenable to formalization and precision, development may nonetheless be characterized as a series of resting places— "approximations" Browning, like Carlyle, calls them—which are the best attainable at a given time but which eventually prove inadequate. The quest for conditional accommodations for what the poet characteristically calls "soul" is discernible throughout his work, from the "principle of restlessness" iterated in his first published poem (*Pauline* [1833], l. 277) to his belief in striving in the afterlife spoken of in his last ("Epilogue" to *Asolando*.)[1]

Early on, Browning had envisioned his career as a kind of pilgrimage on the road to the Absolute, his poems being stages providing points of departure for the next steps forward. He was fully aware, however, that the Absolute would never be attained. As he said in his *Essay on Shelley* (1852), in which he cast an oblique glance backward over his own development, it is the business of a poet to behold the universe and all therein "in their actual state of perfection in imperfection" but to look to "the forthcoming stage of man's being" and so suggest "this ideal of a future man," thereby striving "to elevate and extend" both himself and mankind. Of course, Browning hastens to add, "an absolute vision is not for this world, but we are permitted a continual approximation to it." His poems are these approximations, representations of life whose progress toward the Absolute is determined by their own inadequacies. One representation or form of consciousness fails and another is chosen to take its place. Yet the new representation is not in any way a deductive necessity, nor are the connections entailments: Browning recognizes that there could always be different starting points and different routes taken to arrive at provisional ends.

Although in his poems written prior to his marriage in 1846 Browning had worked out his own philosophy and artistic creed in light of his embrace of the doctrine of becoming (and in *Sordello* [1840] especially had arrived at an almost perfect example of the romantic ironic art of symphilosophy and sympoetry that Schlegel had envisioned[2]), he had not specifically addressed the subject of religious belief in this way. In such poems as "Saul" (published incomplete in 1845) he had begun to examine his inherited Christian faith, but as his inability to finish "Saul" would seem to indicate, he still had further to go.

By the mid-1840s Browning could affirm the intervention of the Absolute in history and accept the Incarnation as a mythic pattern for self-realization and as a model of organization for his life as artist; he agreed with his future wife that Christianity is a "worthy *myth,* & poetically acceptable" (Kintner, 1:43). In his discussions and correspondence with Elizabeth Barrett in 1845–46, when the subject of religion arose from time to time, it mainly concerned the observances and forms of worship Christianity may take. She confessed, fairly early in their acquaintance, that she was from a dissenting background although not really interested in sectarianism as such, "hating as I do . . . all that rending of the garment of Christ, . . . & caring very little for most dogmas & doxies in themselves . . . & believing that there is only one church in heaven & earth, with the one divine High Priest to it" (Kintner, 1:141). In reply Browning acknowledged that he too was from a dissenting family but did not elaborate other than to say that this was not a "point of disunion" between them (Kintner, 1:143). A year later the pair again turned to the question of sectarianism, and in explanation of her position Elizabeth Barrett spoke of her unwillingness "to put on any of the liveries of the sects" (Kintner, 2:962). Browning agreed:

> Look at the injunction to "love God with all the heart, and soul, and strength"—and then imagine yourself bidding any faculty, that arises towards the love of him, be still! If in a meeting house, with the blank white walls, and a simple doctrinal exposition,—all the senses should turn (from where they lie neglected) to all that sunshine in the Sistine with its music and painting, which would lift them at once to Heaven,—why should you not go forth?

And then, after an elaborate metaphor, Browning continues:

> See the levity! No—this sort of levity only exists because of the strong conviction, I do believe! There seems no longer need of earnestness in assertion, or proof . . so it runs lightly over, like foam on the top of a wave. (Kintner, 2:969)

Browning's treatment of the subject here is instructive, for it is typically Browningesque: having addressed a serious subject directly and sincerely, he then withdraws and resorts to "levity."

This is, as we shall see, exactly the procedure in the first poem of any length written after his marriage.

Browning composed "Christmas-Eve," said to be a central document in the poet's religious history,[3] in late 1849 or early 1850, after the birth of his son and the subsequent death of his mother, which threw him into a profound depression from which he did not soon recover. It was perhaps inevitable that, reflecting on his feeling of desolation following his mother's death so soon after the experience of extreme joy at the birth of his son, the poet should turn to religion as the subject of his next poem. Indeed, the passages on death (ll. 1211–27) and hope for an afterlife (ll. 350–72) are probably the core of "Christmas-Eve," around which was clustered the complex dream vision dealing with different modes of worship.

Touched as he was personally by the facts of birth and death, Browning no doubt wished to heed his wife's early advice to write a moral and religious poem in which he spoke in his own voice (Kintner, 1:14–16). Yet when he thought of elaborating the core passages of his poem into considerations of modes of worship more or less along the lines of their earlier correspondence, he found he could not "speak out" in this instance any more than he could do so earlier. Possibly he conceived of the device of the dream vision as a means of distancing himself from his material. But upon reflection even this would, in the end, mean pinning himself down to a certain stance, and being Browning, he would not preclude possibility. The only way out was, then, the way he had adopted earlier, especially in *Sordello,* and the way he had dealt with Elizabeth Barrett's remarks on sectarianism: namely, narrative informed by "levity." I wish to suggest that the imaginative donnée of "Christmas-Eve" is not, *pace* the many commentators on Browning's religious beliefs, modes of worship or even the Christian faith, but romantic irony.

The poem, published in 1850 as the first part of *Christmas-Eve and Easter-Day,* is a dramatic narrative of events that befell a certain unnamed speaker on Christmas Eve, 1849. To whom it is addressed is never made clear; indeed, the speaker's notion of his audience, his way of dealing with it, and the verb tense of his narrative change. To escape the rain he enters a dissenting chapel, in which an ugly and mean congregation are preached to by an ignorant, bigoted man. He withdraws to the open air, where he congratulates himself upon his own (superior) mode of worship, which entails direct communication with the divine without any kind of earthly mediation. Suddenly a rainbow appears and from it issues forth what seems to be the figure of Christ (although he is never named), who gathers the speaker up in his white robe (or, to be exact, the robe gathers him up) and transports him on a magical mystery tour to Rome, where he witnesses the midnight mass at St. Peter's, and to Göttingen, where he hears a lecturer (who obviously espouses the Higher Criticism) demythologize the Christian story.[4] Noting that Christ had apparently been present in the chapel and had entered into the observances at both Rome and Göttingen, the speaker eventually admits that there are many perceptions of truth and that each person's realization of it is true for him if for no one else, whereupon he finds himself back in the chapel and returned to ordinary consciousness. He questions the reality of the experience, although feeling certain that something unusual has happened to him, and decides that he will continue in that way of worship which employs fewest earthly aids but that he will not henceforth deny to other modes their own validity. Hence, instead of "attacking the choice of my neighbors round, / With none of my own made—I choose here!" (ll. 1340–41). Although the people gathered in the chapel are just as unprepossessing as before, the narrator recognizes the water of life in their earthen vessel and joins them here in their way, which he believes is but one of many ways to truth.

This is borne out by the imagery of the robe and the rainbow. The robe first appears when the speaker attests to the power and beauty of God. What he sees, however, is only the garment, "vast and white, / With a hem that I could recognize" (ll. 438–39). Significantly, he never looks directly at the face of the figure in the robe, nor does he embrace the figure directly but holds by the hem or is swept up in the folds of the vesture. Truth, as Browning constantly reiterates, can never be apprehended, only aspects of it perceived. As he was to say in the *Essay on Shelley,* written less than two years after "Christmas-Eve," although we can never reach the Absolute, we can have approximations of it. But what kind of approximation? A mythus, a provisional system or conception, something never fully to be believed in but to be embraced as a structure of belief. As Schlegel said, "It is equally fatal for the mind to have a system or to have none. It will therefore have to combine both" (*A* 53, *KA* 2:173).

The lunar rainbow, "vast and perfect / From heaven to heaven extending," rises "with its seven proper colors chorded" until they coalesce into the "whitest white" (ll. 385–93). White is of course made up of all colors, and it is here used to suggest that truth is characterized by many aspects and may be approached in many ways. It is, the speaker comprehends, perhaps permissible to pursue *my* way but only with the understanding that my way is not the only way.

Formally the narrative, which is carefully organized, would appear to underscore the seriousness of the speaker's understanding about the nature of truth. In structure it is circular, with an introduction and a coda. Yet the effect is not of careful organization but of cramming and stuffing, of fantasy and unreality. Many passages have little to do with modes of worship but, for example, with the Incarnation itself in the scene at Rome and the need for accepting the divinity of Christ in the scene at Göttingen. In short, "Christmas-Eve" seems something of a grab bag. This effect is heightened by the verse form—Hudibrastics that lend a tone of grotesquerie and facetiousness to content often of intense seriousness. In other words, the poem is an excellent example of the arabesque—an artfully arranged confusion of symmetry and chaos—and with its "transcendental buffoonery" it is permeated by the irony that suggests the insoluble conflict between the absolute and the relative, the necessity and yet the impossibility of total communication.

Browning makes sure to leave us with no notion that this is

his final word on the subject of modes of worship: in fact, he causes us to wonder whether this dream vision has even been a serious consideration of the subject. First, the speaker questions the reality of the experience: if, in fact, he has been transported to various parts of the world, how is it that he has heard the sermon in the chapel and been able to note in detail all its deficiencies: "How else was I found there, bolt upright / On my bench, as if I had never left it?" (ll. 1238–39). Second, the speaker admits to "levity" in his treatment of the matter, this in no small part owing to language itself, which does not permit adequate discussion of the infinite because of its finite nature:

> Lest myself, at unawares, be found,
>   While attacking the choice of my neighbors round,
> With none of my own made—I choose here!
> The giving out of the hymn reclaims me;
> I have done: and if any blames me,
> Thinking that merely to touch in brevity
>   The topics I dwell on, were unlawful,—
> Or worse, that I trench, with undue levity,
>   On the bounds of the holy and awful,—
> I praise the heart, and pity the head of him,
> And refer myself to THEE, instead of him,
> Who head and heart alike discernest,
>   Looking below light speech we utter,
>   When frothy spume and frequent sputter
> Prove that the soul's depths boil in earnest!
>
>   (ll. 1339–53)

Third, the poem ends with a complete violation of the pretense that this has been a dramatic poem, as the speaker says:

> I have done: . . .
> I put up pencil and join chorus
> To Hepzibah Tune, without further apology. . . .
>   (ll. 1343, 1355–56)

This has been no fictional character speaking: it is the poet writing. "The giving out of the hymn reclaims me" (l. 1342), recalls him from fantasy to present actuality; and so, in a remarkable example of parabasis and aesthetic play, the poet reveals that this has been a poetic and thus fanciful exercise as he decides to "put up pencil" (l. 1355). In effect, Browning tells us that this is not a presentation or even a re-presentation of experience but is in fact a poem, not life but art. And hovering above the poem is the figure of the poet, like Thackeray's Manager of the Performance, smiling at his creation and partaking of it, being both immanent and transcendent, as he presents us with a poem that is self-conscious and self-regarding—that is, aware of itself as art.

Yet what we are left with in the end is not simply a work of art in which the poet hovers above the poem and glorifies in his own self-activity. For at the close Browning, who believed that the poet's business is with God,[5] looks beyond those who might blame him for levity to "refer myself to THEE" and yet at the same time joins in the fellowship of hymn singing. Displaying both the transcendental and descendental thrusts of his nature, the poet seems to suggest that at least one way of getting to the figure of Christ is through the experience of him as it is mediated in the historical continuity of human fellowship, here represented by the congregation on this Christmas Eve.

As we have seen, in the poem Browning presents four different ways of celebrating the Christmas festival. The first, the way of the dissenters, is characterized by a preaching of biblical literalism, exclusiveness, and a kind of predestination. The second, the narrator's own way, is entirely private and individualistic, eschewing ecclesiastical tradition and authority and supposing an immediate access to the divine without earthly aids. The third way, that of the Roman Catholics, prefers the Gospel fellowship of the Christian church as the unity of the eternal and the historical. The fourth way, that of the Higher Criticism, demythologizes the Christian story but nevertheless venerates the myth of Christ and the supreme greatness of the man Jesus.

Good Victorian ironist that he is, Browning has the shadowy figure of Christ give apparent approval to the most divergent and even contradictory ways of worship as they are informed by various beliefs: they are all what Carlyle called "true fictions," finite (and thus imperfect) formulations of the Infinite. The poet here dramatizes his belief that no religious or philosophical point of view, no conceptual framework, no demonstrative proof can ever be adequate by itself. For every premise there is a context and a set of propositions taken for granted. For every argument there is a perspective unchallenged. For every moral or religious principle there are a social milieu, a set of cultural needs, and a history that makes such exercises intelligible and plausible. Like Foucault later, Browning (although within an idealist framework) recognizes the reality of imprisonment, the incarceration of human beings within systems of thought and practice that have become so much a part of them that they do not experience these systems as a series of confinements but embrace them as the very structure of being human. In sum, the poet dramatizes his view that all embodiments are imperfect but necessary (because they are all one has to work with).

The Christ in this poem is sentient of how the various "ways" have been produced, and he is forgiving, indeed approving of them all save that of the speaker's, which is private, noncommunal and noncommunicative, and therefore approaching (to borrow Kierkegaard's term) "infinite absolute negativity."[6] As a result of his dream vision the narrator seems to learn that only corporate worship has Christ's blessing. But, pondering the other ways, the speaker is uncertain which is the one for him: "Needs must there be one way, our chief / Best way of worship?" he asks (ll. 1170–71). The answer is no. For as Browning's Sordello learned, "the real way seemed made up of all the ways" (*Sordello*, 6:36). Still, being finite and limited, one cannot embrace all the ways: one must choose. And so, evidencing the self-assertion and the self-restriction of the romantic ironist as he aims for communality and communication, the speaker says, "I choose here!" (l. 1341). Here, because one is here, in a community of believers. Whether they are congenial souls is neither here nor there: they are "my neighbors" (l. 1340), the other to whom I must open out and thus experience the joy of the Christmas festival.

The monologist discovers what Browning was constantly concerned to portray: namely, that everything has meaning. Phenomena, myriad and diverse as they are, are all parts of a whole. Fragmentation, discontinuity, ugliness, evil—these are readily discernible even to the most unpracticed eye. It is the artist's business however to show how they fit into the whole. For the artist is what is called in *Sordello* the "Maker-see." By uncovering what has been hidden, by defamiliarizing what has been dulled by the blindness of custom, by lifting phenomena out of the field of ordinary perception and placing them within a network of relationships that constitute the work of art—by so doing the artist makes his readers experience the becoming of an object in the boundless universe of change. To Browning, development, advance on the road to the Absolute, entails engaging in the thought of the other, the different and the alien; it is the process of endeavoring to experience alterity and to examine to what extent it is possible to think differently, instead of legitimating that which is already known. And so to show his joy in his discovery of this unprepossessing congregation's meaning and value, the speaker (who is soon to be revealed as an artist) embraces the fellowship and joins in the hymn "without further apology" (l. 1356).

But is this Browning's final word in the poem? Surely not. For if this, or something like it, is taken as the poet's last word, then certainty takes precedence over possibility: the irony of the poem is to be relegated to the camp of Wayne C. Booth and the reconstructionists. But, as is always the case with Browning, there is more to say. With him, as with other romantic ironists, any affirmation is only provisional, is only a proximate formulation of truth. His irony does not allow the subject to come to a stop at a single point but causes it to travel incessantly between

the finite and the infinite, the bounded and the free, the signifier
and the signified; it is a balance of dialectical movement. In the
end "Christmas-Eve" is, as the speaker says, "reclaimed"—reclaimed from fixity for becoming. The last word belongs to the
poet, who, interrupting his narrative and turning to his audience,
insists as he puts up his pencil that the imaginative donnée of his
poem is romantic irony.

It is then a vain endeavor to look to "Christmas-Eve"—or to
any other of Browning's poems, for that matter—for final state-
ments of the poet's religious beliefs. Mrs. Sutherland Orr, who
knew Browning personally and well and who is one of the few
critics to deal perspicaciously with his religious views, remarked
that the poet's religious belief "held a saving clause, which re-
moved it from all dogmatic . . . grounds of controversy: the more
definite or concrete conceptions of which it consists possessed no
finality for even his own mind; they represented for him an absolute truth in contingent relations to it."[7] Other critics have, however, been less percipient and have bedeviled the poem to extract a
statement of Browning's religious creed. Those commentators
who, for example, view "Christmas-Eve" as the poet's evaluation
of the relative merits of the three modes of worship and as "his
decision in favor of the Dissenting Chapel, for the Chapel seems
in the poet's opinion to have received most fittingly the gift of
God's Son to the world,"[8] have failed to perceive, among other
things, that neither the speaker's dream vision nor the modes of
worship lie at the imaginary heart of the poem. They not only stop
too soon, with "I choose here!" (l. 1341), and thereby overlook
the last eighteen lines, but they also fail to perceive that in Browning's world meaning is always in the making, man is always
making and unmaking himself, the individual is, like the race,
always in a state of becoming.

If there is a "way" in the poem, it is the way of levity's
rainbow, yielding not creeds but fictions of faith. Browning can
wholeheartedly embrace the rainbow, the Bible's image of cove-
nant, as it is revealed to him in his place- and time-bound situa-

tion; for him it has existential meaning as the best "image" of truth available for the time being. Yet it is, in the last analysis, but an image, a sign, not the thing itself. It is a rainbow, literally a refraction and a reflection, informed by the Absolute which it cannot contain. As the Higher Critics would put it, it is a myth. Thus it is a provisional truth, and the chapel where the speaker in the poem finds himself is but a conditional accommodation. Like all embodiments in Browning's world it can never be a final "image." And so to indicate its provisional nature, the speaker resorts to levity, a kind of Kierkegaardian humor that does not mock the religious content but serves to underscore it.[9] "Christmas-Eve" is but the first of Browning's poems, like "A Death in the Desert" and *The Ring and the Book,* that scrutinize the nature of religious myth and, with regard to it, ask: what will suffice?

4

THE CHAMELEON PERSONALITY
Arnold's Poetry

While critics frequently speak of the irony in Browning's work, they do not often associate the term with the poetry of Matthew Arnold. Instead, critics such as Lionel Trilling more often comment on Arnold's "sincerity"; and even when they perceive a certain irony in his work, it is to his prose and not to his poetry that they look. Douglas Bush, for example, in his book on Arnold, allows that "although he was to become a master of irony in prose, he rarely approached it in verse."[1] Yet almost every contemporary account that we have about the man, from early youth to the time of his death, testifies to his playfulness, his posturings, his poses. Many of his friends and family were surprised that he was even capable of the seriousness that they discovered in his first published volume of poems. And later, when his seriousness was no longer to be questioned, his readers were often amazed by the levity that frequently seemed to invade his work. In his autobiography the philologist Max Mueller noted that Arnold "trusts . . . to *persiflage,* and the result was that when he tried to be serious, people could not forget that he might at any time turn round and smile, and decline to be *au grand serieux.*"[2] Jest and seriousness, artless openness and dissimulation—these seem to have been the characteristics of Arnold the man. They were also the same qualities that define his poetry.

60

In Arnold's world all is in course of change. Characterized by an endless process of creation and de-creation, nature in its plentitude is always in a state of becoming, everything being both itself and something else. In this world the individual, seeing that *a* is both *a* and *a becoming b,* faces contradictions on all sides; and this perception engenders the most contradictory impulses within himself, the desire for, simultaneously, fixity and fluidity, involvement and detachment, subjectivity and objectivity, bondage and freedom. Further, the self recognizes its own instability, its essential nothingness. "I am nothing," Arnold wrote to his friend Arthur Clough, "and very probably never shall be anything—but there are characters which are truest to themselves by never being anything, when circumstances do not suit."[3] And speaking of his poems to his sister Jane, Arnold urged: "Fret not yourself to make my poems square in all their parts. . . . The true reason why parts suit you while others do not is that my poems are fragments—*i.e.* that I am fragments. . . ; the whole effect of my poems is quite vague & indeterminate. . . ; & do not plague yourself to find a consistent meaning. . . ."[4] His was, he confessed to Clough, a chameleon personality: "I can go thro: the imaginary process of mastering myself and see the whole affair as it would then stand, but at the critical point I am too apt to hoist up the mainsail to the wind and let her drive" (*Letters to Clough,* p. 110). For like Goethe, he was quite willing to believe that in most matters "there is no certainty, but alternating dispositions" (*Letters to Clough,* p. 86). Yes, "this little which we are / Swims on an obscure much we might have been." One cannot "talk of *the* absolutely right but of *a* promising method with ourselves" (*Letters to Clough,* p. 85). "'Hide thy life,' said Epicurus, and the exquisite zest there is in doing so can only be appreciated by those who, desiring to introduce some method into their lives, have suffered from the malicious pleasure the world takes in trying to distract them till they are as shatter-brained and empty-hearted as the world itself."[5] Years later Arnold was to claim the chameleon personality as the ideal critic: "The critic of poetry should have the finest tact, the nicest moderation, the most free, flexible, and elastic spirit imaginable; he should be indeed the 'ondoyant et divers,' the *undulating and diverse* being of Montaigne."[6]

An undulating and diverse being, one given to aesthetic and metaphysical play—this is the hallmark of Arnold the poet, especially in his early verses, where he assumes a number of stances and presents varying positions all of which are deemed of equal value. Let us consider the matter of fate, for example, in *The Strayed Reveller and Other Poems* (1849). Poem after poem deals with characters as victims of fate, yet in almost every case the working of fate is called into question. "Mycerinus" considers whether there is a "Force" that makes all "slaves of a tyrannous necessity," or whether the gods are "mere phantoms of man's self-tormenting heart" (ll. 42, 25).[7] The chorus in the "Fragment of an 'Antigone' " praises both those who flee from fate and those who observe its dictates. The eager response of "To a Republican Friend" is mitigated in "Continued" by the "uno'erleaped Mountains of Necessity, / Sparing us narrower margin than we deem." The laborer in "The World and the Quietist" is granted a sense of omnipotence although his and others' actions are limited by how "Fate decreed." The speaker in "Written in Emerson's Essays" contends that "the will is free," so "Gods are we, bards, saints, heroes, if we will"; but the last line of the poem asks whether this be "truth or mockery" (the manuscript reading being the more decisive "O barren boast, o joyless Mockery"). The colloquist in "Resignation" staunchly maintains that persons "who await / No gifts from chance, have conquered fate" (ll. 247–48), while also freely admitting that fate thwarts our expectations of life (ll. 271–78).

This same ambivalence about fate marks the poems of Arnold's later volumes as well. The initial lyrics of the "Switzerland" series assume that the relationship with Marguerite is doomed to fail, and subsequent ones impute the lovers' parting to "a God [who] their severance ruled" ("To Marguerite—Continued," l. 22) because for "durability . . . they were not meant"

("The Terrace at Berne," ll. 43–44). The workings of fate are inexorable: "I knew it when my life was young; / I feel it still, now youth is o'er" (Ibid., ll. 49–50). Communication on the deeper levels of sensibility is impossible because that which seals the lips "hath been deep-ordained," yet occasionally there come moments when we talk openly and sincerely ("The Buried Life," ll. 29, 87). Arnold's speakers are forever questioning whether they are free or determined, and they conclude, hopefully but questioningly, with the possibility that they are both: "Ah, *some* power exists there, which is ours?" ("Self-Deception," l. 27).

Arnold's views of nature are also contradictory. In "Quiet Work," "Lines Written in Kensington Gardens," "A Summer Night," and "The Youth of Man" nature is the great moral exemplar, teaching "toil unsevered from tranquillity" ("Quiet Work"). In "In Harmony with Nature," "The Youth of Nature," "Self-Dependence," and "A Wish," on the other hand, nature is shown to be a distinct realm of being that mankind cannot possibly emulate and would not wish to if it could: "Nature and man can never be fast friends" ("In Harmony with Nature"). No attempt is made to come down on either side of the question, as Arnold presents not certainties but possibilities. Here it is not a matter of either/or but of both/and.

The same may be said of Arnold's many verses dealing with love. In poems like "Dover Beach" and "The Buried Life" love is regarded as redemptive, whereas in the Marguerite poems and "Tristram and Iseult" it is shown to be a snare and delusion. Though love alone appears able to fill the void in which "we mortal millions live *alone*" ("To Marguerite—Cont."), passion, or the love that engenders it, is too unstable, too transient to provide a firm basis for life.

Arnold's favorite situations are those that are intrinsically ironic. Mycerinus, the good king, is condemned to an early death while his father, who spurned justice, lived long and happily. Homer, though blind, saw much ("To a Friend"). Shakespeare, the greatest of poets, "didst tread on earth unguessed at"

("Shakespeare"). The Duke of Wellington, the leader of conservative forces, sponsored revolution but in accordance with law
("To the Duke of Wellington"). The Strayed Reveller "enswines"
himself in Circe's palace, the enchantress having "lured him not
hither" (l. 97).

From basically ironic situations Arnold develops, even in his
earliest poems, narratives of more complex irony. In "A Memory
Picture" lovers' promises are made to be broken and "new
made—to break again" (l. 38). The Modern Sappho waits for her
lover whose attention is now focused on another but who, "as he
drifts to fatigue, discontent, and dejection, / Will be brought,
thou poor heart, how much nearer to thee!" The New Sirens argue
that, "only, what we feel, we know" (l. 84). Yet, because feeling
is evanescent and ignorance the way of life, the speaker, eschewing roses and lilies for cypress and yew, approaches love from a
new point of view: "Shall I seek, that I may scorn her, / Her I
loved at eventide?" (ll. 271–72). In similar fashion the speaker of
"The Voice" hears a compelling voice that issues a "thrilling
summons to my will" and makes "my tossed heart its life-blood
spill," yet to which his will ultimately remains unshaken and his
heart unbroken. On the other hand, the speaker of "To Fausta," in
full realization that joys flee when sought and that dreams are
false and hollow, nevertheless may go in pursuit of them. The
gipsy child has "foreknown the vanity of hope, / Foreseen [his]
harvest—yet proceed[s] to live" ("To a Gipsy Child by the Seashore"). The busy world is made aware of its power only when
reminded of the vanity of its busyness, just as Darius was most
mindful of his power when made aware of the one check to it
("The World and the Quietist").

A number of the early poems dramatize Arnold's perception
that each moment is a watershed "when, equally, the seas of life
and death are fed" ("Resignation," l. 260). This is particularly
true of the verses dealing with moral problems, the point of which
is that the arguments are about as good on one side as another. In
the "Fragment of an 'Antigone' " the chorus is right in its praise

of Antigone, who in respect for universal law buried her brother in violation of the civil law and with disregard to her lover; but Haemon is also right in his claim that Antigone preferred a corpse to her lover. No wonder then that the chorus is forced to conclude that praise is due both him who "makes his own welfare his unswerved-from law" (1. 8) *and* him who "dares / To self-selected good / Prefer obedience to the primal law" (ll. 28–30). In "The Sick King in Bokhara" the vizier is right in his respect for the law and its demand that the individual follow it unswervingly; yet the king is surely not wrong to heed the claims of conscience and seek to mitigate the punishment of the moolah. In "The Forsaken Merman" Margaret is shown to be both right and wrong in her return to land: a wife and mother, she has obligations in the sea world to her family, which she leaves desolate; but a human, she also has responsibilities in the land world, where she must fulfill her religious duties among her kind.

Such poems, which are dramatizations of irony, are reflective of the young poet's embrace of irony as a cosmic view. In the modern world certainty is rarely if ever possible. What is required in confronting such a world, Arnold evidently believes, is an ironic posture that permits toleration of indeterminacy. Thus, whether the poet sees deeply or widely—possibilities entertained in, respectively, "The Strayed Reveller" and "Resignation"—is not easily determined, and both alternatives should be entertained. Thus, whether the universe is of divine or purely physical origin, one should be for either case prepared ("In Utrumque Paratus") or, to use a favorite term of Arnold's, resigned.

Much has been made of Arnold's stoic resignation and his supposedly bleak view of life. But as his Empedocles says, one need not despair if one cannot dream ("Empedocles on Etna," 1.2.423–26). Life is still worth living even though one has "fore-known the vanity of hope" ("To a Gipsy Child"). Often the poet's stoic attitude seems no more than that, an attitude, a posture, a pose. Where Mycerinus was a stoic posing as a reveller, Arnold not infrequently appears to be a reveller posing as a stoic. As a poet he is always exploring possibilities with a tentativeness, a drawing back that does not permit conclusiveness. In his work as in his letters there are constant oscillations while he explores options that receive, even at the moment he seems to embrace them, only provisional assent. The narrator's "It may be" in his examination of Mycerinus' inner self well expresses the poet's own qualified positions; and his explorations are not experiments in despair but, frequently, playful exercises "not of mere resigned acquiescence, not of melancholy quietism, but of joyful activity" (Super, 3:177). As he told Clough, "composition seems to keep alive in me a *cheerfulness*—a sort of Tuchtigkeit [*sic*], or natural soundness and valiancy" (*Letters to Clough,* p. 146). Even in his apparently darkest poems there is something of Mycerinus' "clear laughter . . . ringing through the gloom" (l. 113), issuing from the poet's playful acceptance of the ironic fact that man is born with desires that cannot be fulfilled:

> Why each is striving, from of old,
> To love more deeply than he can?
> Still would be true, yet still grows cold?
> —Ask of the Powers that sport with man!
>
> They yoked in him, for endless strife,
> A heart of ice, a soul of fire;
> And hurled him on the Field of Life,
> An aimless unallayed Desire. ("Destiny")

The "sport" of the gods can be the poet's, and the poet's serious play is illustrative of the belief Arnold shared with Schiller that "lofty thought lies oft in childish play" ("Thekla's Answer").

The poems of *Empedocles on Etna and Other Poems* (1852) portray characters playing out their roles in complex dramas of undefined irony. Let us look, for example, at "The Church of Brou." To memorialize her dead husband and their love for each other, the duchess erects a church and inside it an ornate tomb, on the top of which are effigies of the pair lying side by side.

Eventually, she too is buried in this tomb. Centuries pass while the dead lovers are left alone in their church, undisturbed except for Sunday services. The meaning of their memorial is now forgotten as people after mass visit the tomb "and marvel at the Forms of stone, / And praise the chiseled broideries rare" until they part and "the princely Pair are left alone / In the Church of Brou" (2.36–40). Here in this lonely sepulchre there is no life, only the silent art of glass and stone. Wishing them well the narrator apostrophizes: "So sleep, for ever sleep, O marble Pair!" (3.16). And then momentarily indulging in the dream of eternal love that might have been theirs, or what at the instant might be his, he considers two possibilities of their awaking: first, when the western sun shines through the stained glass and throws a dazzling array of colors throughout the church and they will say, *"What is this? we are in bliss—forgiven— / Behold the pavement of the courts of Heaven!"*; or second, when the autumn rains come and the moon occasionally shines out and through the windows of the clerestory illuminates the "foliaged marble forest" and they will say, *"This is the glimmering verge of Heaven, and these / The columns of the heavenly palaces!"* (3.30–31, 41–42). This is of course but a fancy, and even in the fancy the lovers would be deluded, because it is not in heaven but in the church of Brou wherein the putatively awakened pair find themselves. The fact is that they continue to lie under "the lichen-crusted leads above" on which there is but the dream of listening to "the rustle of the eternal rain of love." In the long run, art serves neither as a memorial nor a transformation; it remains but beautiful forms at which to marvel.

In poem after poem Arnold recalls us to the fact that what we witness in his verse is not life but art. The action of "Empedocles on Etna" centers on the Sicilian philosopher, but the last word is given to Callicles, who undercuts the poem by stating explicitly that what we have just witnessed is not the proper subject matter for poetry—"Not here, O Apollo! / Are haunts meet for thee" (2.2.421–22)—and by saying pretty much what Arnold himself said in his Preface to the 1853 *Poems* when he explained why he was not reprinting the poem. The separation of the poet from the poem can also be witnessed in the "Stanzas in Memory of the Author of 'Obermann'," wherein after praising the author and his book the poet bids farewell to both: "I go, fate drives me; but I leave / Half of my life with you" (ll. 132–33). In such verses the poet, like God, is both in and out of his creation, subjective and objective, immanent and transcendent. He "moves, but never moveth on" ("The Hayswater Boat").

Although doubleness and dividedness are commonplaces of Victorian literature, the degree of self-reflexivity in Arnold is uncommon. Arnold is always splitting himself up into various "selves"—the best self and the ordinary self, the buried self and the masked self. On the one hand, modern life with its constant claims and banalities calling us out of ourselves necessitates this; on the other hand, the ennui of solitude and the fear that there is no real self at all compel such a separation. "Two desires" toss the poet about: "One drives him to the world without, / And one to solitude" ("Stanzas in Memory of the Author of 'Obermann'," ll. 93–96). "And I," puzzles the speaker of "A Summer Night," "I know not if to pray / Still to be what I am, / Or yield and be / Like all the other men I see" (ll. 34–36). The answer is clearly that he will have to be both.

The inadequacy of language, its inability to permit one to delve into oneself and express what is there or what is lacking, in part mandates the answer. Arnold perhaps best explores language's deficiencies in "The Buried Life," in which the speaker and his beloved, though engaging in a "war of mocking words," cannot communicate openly. Love is apparently too weak to open the heart and let it speak, yet the desire remains to apprehend the buried life and to share it with another. After investigating the impossibility of such communication, the speaker, seemingly unmindful of the presence of his beloved, then says that it is possible: "When a belovéd hand is laid in ours, / . . . / The eye sinks inward, and the heart lies plain, / And what we mean, we say, and what we would, we know" (ll. 78, 86–87). This seems to be but hypothetical, however, because the nature and destiny of the buried self are not revealed. Further, in looking into his beloved's eyes he sees himself mirrored there: his eye sinks inward and he becomes aware of *his* life's flow and *thinks* he knows where his life rose and where it goes.

What the speaker discovers about the buried life is that which cannot be said. Silence is all that is possible in consideration of the great questions of life. Thus the models Arnold holds up for emulation can be both superhuman—like Shakespeare and the poet of "Resignation"—or subhuman—like the gipsies of "Resignation" and the gipsy child—but they have one trait in common: they do not or cannot break their silence to offer any counsel. It is each person's own impossible struggle to find the right words. Man has the letters God has given him to "make with them what word he could." Different civilizations have combined them in different ways and "something was made." But man knows that "he has not yet found the word God would." If only he could achieve the right words in the right order, then he would be relieved of a terrible oppression and at long last breathe free ("Revolutions"). But this will never happen: human language belongs to the phenomenal world and it can never encompass the noumenal world to speak God's word. The poet, Arnold knows, can never fully replicate or re-present anything. That is why it must always be admitted "that the singer was less than his themes." No, even the best of poets—"who have read / Most in themselves—have beheld / Less than they left unrevealed" ("The Youth of Nature," ll. 89, 104–6). The truth is that the buried self cannot be expressed because without the proper words it cannot be apprehended.

To attempt to view their inner being from various perspectives, Arnold's heroes don masks and play roles, just as Arnold did when he assumed the role of dandy in the late 1840s. And with their roles and masks they not only view themselves but also become spectators watching others watching themselves watch

others. To refuse to engage in this kind of dramatic play is, in the
mid-nineteenth century at any rate, to admit to inelasticity, to be
spiritually moribund: "only death / Can cut his oscillations short,
and so / Bring him to poise" ("Empedocles," 2.232–34). Poise,
peace, rest, calm—those qualities that speaker after speaker
claims to desire: these are, Arnold knows, the attributes of death:

> 'Tis death! and peace, indeed, is here . . . .
> But is a calm like this, in truth,
> The crowning end of life and youth,
> And when this boon rewards the dead,
> Are all debts paid, has all been said?

The answer is a ringing no: *"Calm's not life's crown, though
calm is well. /* 'Tis all perhaps which man acquires, / But 'tis not
what our youth desires" ("Youth and Calm"). In Arnold's world
there is always more to say; there are always visions to be revised.

After 1852 most of Arnold's better poems were written in the
elegiac mode. Elegy was a congenial mode for him because it
allowed for the irony of reversal:[8] Lycidas is dead and we lament
his loss as we celebrate his talents; but Lycidas is not dead, he
lives on in another state. As Arnold employed it, his poems in this
mode call into question the meaning of their opening parts. We
see this clearly in "The Scholar-Gipsy." The poem begins by
building up the myth of the scholar-gipsy to the point where the
narrator himself asserts the living reality of the young Oxonian of
two hundred years ago: "Have I not passed thee . . .?" (l. 123).
But then this assertion in the form of a question is almost immediately denied: "But what—I dream! . . . [T]hou from earth art
gone / Long since, and in some quiet churchyard laid" (ll. 131,
136–37). The scholar is indeed dead, and the verbs associated
with him change to the past tense. However, this is but momentary, for while talking of how the scholar fled with his powers
unsullied and undiverted to the world, the speaker again resurrects
him and speaks of him in the present tense: "Thou waitest for the

spark from heaven" (l. 171). It is an imaginative recovery: the speaker grants him "an immortal lot," because he "imagine[s] thee exempt from age" (ll. 157–58). But immortal lot or not, the scholar is still apparently subject to the ills that afflict mortals living nowadays. And so if he is ever to encounter the divine spark, the scholar must flee the infection of modern life to which present-day mortals are subject and, like the Tyrian trader, establish his enterprise elsewhere.

The poem complicates itself still further by purportedly dealing with two quests that are in fact one and the same: the speaker's quest for the scholar-gipsy and the scholar's for some kind of revelation. Although the scholar quests for the secret knowledge of nature, which can be gained only by nonrational means, he himself is already the embodiment of that knowledge. For the poet makes him a kind of nature-spirit, who, in the first part of the poem, can be perceived only by the simple and untutored or by those, like poets, who live imaginatively, and who near the end of the poem is granted life "on some mild pastoral slope" listening "with enchanted ears" to nightingales (ll. 216–20). In sum, the scholar is the object of his own quest. And the speaker, questing for the scholar and the secret possessed by him, locates within himself the imaginative insight that the scholar embodies, which is to say that the speaker is the object of his own quest.

If all the elements seem to cancel each other out, what finally are we left with? In the end we are left with the poet himself, who in the elaborate simile concluding the poem reminds us that this is not a transcription of life with its sick hurry, or of nature with its pale pink convolvulus, but art—a poem, a making, over which looms the figure of the poet himself. In the end we see that the imaginative donnée of the poem is not the scholar-gipsy and his quest, or modern life with its ills, or meaning of any kind; rather, it is—as it was for Browning in "Christmas-Eve"—romantic irony, which permits the poet to rise above his finite subject matter to a realm of aesthetic consciousness.

The coda of "Sohrab and Rustum" also serves to recall the

reader from the poem to the poet. In this narrative of ironic situations two persons longing for union are frustrated in that desire and come together only through conflict. When one slays the other, the dead son is transformed into art: first, when he makes himself known by the vermilion seal, which is compared to "some clear porcelain vase" painstakingly made by a Chinese workman for the emperor; and second, when over his grave a giant pillar is erected, which also serves as a seal not only of the son but of the father too in that those who see it say, "*Sohrab, the mighty Rustum's son, lies there, / Whom his great father did in ignorance kill*" (ll. 792–93). In the end Arnold makes of the concluding symbol of the Oxus the same use as Rustum made of the tomb erected for his son. It "seals" the narrative into art and reminds the reader of its maker, saying in effect: "'Sohrab and Rustum,' a poem, Matthew Arnold *fecit.*" Its composition was an exercise in the development of aesthetic consciousness, and as a result the consciousness of the poet, like the winding River Oxus, spirals toward its "luminous home" (l. 890).

Arnold's twistings and turnings in his memorial poems are remarkable in the "Stanzas in Memory of Edward Quillinan." While his friend was alive, the speaker wished him health, success, and fame—qualities that are their own reward, "leave no good behind," and "oftenest make us hard, / Less modest, pure, and kind." But the dead man did not receive them, and thus he was "a man unspoiled." Implicit in the tribute is the notion that Quillinan is therefore better dead than alive: "Alive, we would have changed his lot, / We would not change it now."

In "Haworth Churchyard," the elegy for Charlotte Brontë and prematurely for Harriet Martineau, Arnold followed the usual elegiac reversal of awakening when the poem was first published in 1855:

> Sleep, O cluster of friends,
> Sleep!—or only when May,
> Brought by the west-wind, returns

Back to your native heaths,
And the plover is heard on the moors,
Yearly awake to behold
The opening summer, the sky,
The shining moorland—to hear
The drowsy bee, as of old,
Hum o'er the thyme, the grouse
Call from the heather in bloom!
Sleep, or only for this
Break your united repose!

(ll. 112–24)

When the poem appeared in revised form in 1877, Arnold added an Epilogue, which is nothing less than a palinode. Denying the possibility of a May awakening, the Muse angrily shakes her head and says that this shall not be: these "unquiet souls" will not awaken but will remain "in the dark fermentation of earth," "the never idle workshop of nature," "the eternal movement" of the universe of becoming, and there "ye shall find yourselves again!" (ll. 125–28).

With even less cordiality Arnold elegizes Heinrich Heine in "Heine's Grave," a short study of the kind of ironist that Arnold wished not to be, of "infinite absolute negativity," such as Kierkegaard falsely accused Friedrich Schlegel of being. Heine was of course an ironist, says Arnold, but he lacked love and charm, a concern for others, a real desire to communicate or sympathize with his fellows; and his irony was in consequence bitter. Properly situated in Montmartre Cemetery in Paris and not in Naples' bay or among Ravenna's pines or by the Avon's side, where poets like Virgil, Dante, and Shakespeare belong, Heine's grave reeks of a kind of poison distilled from the harshness and malignity of his life. Once the poet had admired the dead man, but it was necessary that he part from Heine lest he be infected by his scornful laughter. Obviously Arnold has come to re-bury Heine and not to praise him. Yet near the end of his elegy, after 198 lines of mocking derision of the German writer, the poet decides not thus to take leave of him but "with awe / Hail, as it passes from earth / Scattered lightnings, that soul!" (ll. 203–5). At the very end however the poet returns to himself as he asks "the Spirit of the world" to grant that "a life / Other and milder be mine" and that his work be made "a beat of thy joy!" (ll. 225–26, 232). It is evident that what Arnold repudiates in Heine is not his irony but his lack of playfulness, love and joy, an ethical concern characteristic of a higher irony.

In "Thyrsis" Arnold is again critical of the subject to be elegized. Clough-Thyrsis was a "too quick despairer" who deserted the landscape of the scholar-gipsy's haunts by his own will, and because of the storms of which "he could not wait their passing, he is dead" (ll. 61, 50). It is as though Thyrsis, out of silly impatience, had willed his own death, leaving the speaker here alone in these fields that "our Gipsy-Scholar haunts, outliving thee" (l. 197). Yes, the scholar-gipsy remains "a wanderer still; then why not me?" Why not indeed? And so the speaker and the scholar go off, as fellow questers, seeking for the light of truth and apparently putting Thyrsis, the deserter, out of mind. This is, however, an elegy in memory of his friend, and Arnold cannot afford to leave the matter at this point. Adding three final stanzas to the poem, he allows that Thyrsis too was bound on a like quest though in foreign territory. Further, he gives Thyrsis the last word. But addressed to the poet, it urges him to wander on in *his* quest, thereby in the end returning the focus of the poem to the poet himself who hovers above the work.

From this survey of Arnold's poetry we see many of the conflicts that the poet faced and found unresolvable. He was well aware of "wandering between two worlds" ("Stanzas from the Grande Chartreuse," l. 85) and being caught between at least "two desires" ("Stanzas in Memory of the Author of 'Obermann' ") and of the impossibility for him to take either side or bring them into accord. So much about Arnold has long been clear. But what has not been clear is the degree to which Arnold exhibits his conflicts ironically—so as to transcend them. Far from being the poet of "sincerity," Arnold is self-conscious, seriously playful, problematic, and equivocal. His is, in sum, the art of the romantic ironist that presents a self always in process and always relishing and extolling its own self-activity.

5

THE "MONONYMITY"
OF *BLEAK HOUSE*

Much of Dickens's early fiction registers the author's suspicion of change and his advocacy of the values of the past. The year 1848, the year of revolutions, marks a transmutation in his thinking, as in *Dombey and Son* he shows himself fully in favor of social change while at the same time indicating that true salvation rests not with society but with individuals and the domestic affections.[1] This attitude is likewise evident in *David Copperfield,* published over the next two years (1849–50). It is in *Bleak House,* however, that Dickens first anatomizes a whole society and shows its inhabitants imprisoned by the past, for it is in this novel of 1852–53 that Dickens forswears belief in an evolutionary, teleological doctrine of becoming and instead—like Carlyle, who sees islands of cosmos forever arising from and then sinking into chaos—embraces becoming as a process of endless change.

As is generally acknowledged, *Bleak House* is the first of the so-called dark novels belonging to the second half of Dickens's career.[2] Where earlier his fiction was generally optimistic in tone, being the expression of one who seemed to believe in a benign universe in which the aspiring individual could improve himself both morally and physically, during the early 1850s his vision began to darken. On the one hand, he saw society as not only sick but also, in the words of his biographer Edgar Johnson, doomed to

"complete annihilation."[3] No longer was it a matter of ameliora-
tion of social ills, suggested by the coming of the railroad, the
great symbol of social transformation, in *Dombey and Son;* now it
required a total transformation of society following upon explo-
sion and extinction. On the other hand, he witnessed every day
individual acts of benevolence and altruism (such as these per-
formed by his friend Angela Burdett Coutts) that seemed to indicate mankind's natural goodness and to suggest that, under certain
conditions, society could be improved short of dissolution and
rebirth. Which view was correct? As he reflected on the question,
Dickens decided that neither one nor the other was correct but that
both were true.[4] And having arrived at this conclusion—that his
drive toward chaos was as strong as his drive toward order—he
decided to cast his next novel in a form radically different from
that of his previous fiction. He elected to present not one but two
narratives, two different and discordant points of view expressed
by two narrators, and to give priority to neither. The reader would
be left to make up his mind about which view was true or to
accept, like the author, the indeterminacy of the fiction. In settling
on a novel expressive not of either/or but of both/and, Dickens
showed himself a romantic ironist.[5]

"In Bleak House, I have purposely dwelt upon the romantic
side of familiar things," Dickens says in his preface to the novel.
Presumably the romantic side is Esther Summerson's,[6] for Esther's first-person narrative presents a world of health, love, and
order. Hers is the Apollonian view of existence; in a plain, matter-
of-fact style Esther speaks, in the past tense, for stasis, being. She
is within the story, and her subjective point of view is one of
contraction into the enclosed, man-made world represented by
Bleak House, which at the end becomes even smaller, the miniaturized house in Yorkshire. Generically her narrative is a novel-
istic romance.

The other side—the "unromantic," familiar side—belongs
to the nameless narrator. The world he sees is one of disease,
distrust, and disorder, the world of Tom-all-Alone's. In a lively,

extravagant style characterized by a dense poetic texture he speaks, in the historical present tense, for change, for chaos, for a world of ontological becoming. His is the Dionysian view of life. Outside the story, which he tells in the third person, he can go anywhere, but he does not know many of the thoughts and feelings of the characters about whom he speaks. Where Esther experiences and shares the warmth and feeling of domesticity, of love and friendship, the nameless narrator sees mainly the dark surfaces and sordid trappings in a milieu of power plays. Even though his more objective point of view is one of expansion, he primarily focuses on individuals leading desperate lives in an unfeeling world where they must remain alien and apart. It is telling that Esther does not appear within his narrative, whereas Tulkinghorn, the anaesthetic modern man, the very type of power, does not appear within hers. Generically his narrative is an anatomy,[7] a dissection of the dead or dying body of mid-nineteenth-century England.

Dickens divides the sixty-seven chapters of *Bleak House* almost equally between the nameless narrator and Esther, the former having thirty-four and the latter one less. He has the first, she the last. Hers however is not, at least by implication, the last word, for chapter 67, "The Close of Esther's Narrative," terminates not with a full stop but with a long dash, so that the final words of the novel read, "even supposing——— / THE END." There is, thus, no resolution or reconciliation of the two opposing points of view. The "darkness and vacancy" that the nameless narrator sees at the close of his narrative (chapter 66) is by no means enlightened and enlivened by Esther's bright but unfinished summary. It is no wonder that in his working plan for Chapter 67 Dickens wrote: "Wind up. End(?)." For there could not be the kind of end that terminated the conventional novel, because at the close the spheres of the two narrators remain antinomic.[8]

In having his novel recounted by two narrators representing conflicting but apparently equally valid points of view, Dickens, resorting to the paradoxical view of the ironist, was tacitly admitting to the mystery of existence. There are certain things, phenomenal as well as noumenal, he concluded, we can never know. Life is what the case of Jarndyce and Jarndyce is—a "masterly fiction" (pp. 22, 760) constructed by an unknown but master fictioneer. One can expend "study, ability, eloquence, knowledge, intellect" (p. 760) on it, but one can never comprehend it. The fictioneer may provide clues but never answers. From Jo, who "don't know nothink," to Tulkinghorn and Bucket, who seem to know all, the mystery remains impenetrable.

Unlike the nameless narrator, who for all his apparent omniscience has no knowledge of the future, Esther from her partial perspective knows how her story will end. Indeed, her knowledge of the future colors her rendering of the present. She speaks of "the mystery of the future, and the little clue afforded to it by the voice of the present" (p. 69); but in fact the future up to a point well beyond her narrative is certainly known to her. Her position is that of an actor in as well as an observer-reporter of the events she wishes to relate. Constantly apologizing for her prominent part, she says that no matter how hard she tries she cannot keep herself out of it: "I hope any one who may read what I write will understand that if these pages contain a great deal about me, I can only suppose it must be because I have really something to do with them, and can't be kept out" (pp. 102–3). But in spite of herself, it is as an actor, and not as a spectator, that she is more important. For as an observer Esther can see life from but one angle of vision. Although claiming to possess "always a rather noticing way . . . —a silent way of noticing what passed" (p. 17), she often does not understand what she sees: "I saw, but did not comprehend," she admits (p. 713). As readers of her narrative we must necessarily see everything through her eyes; but for the narrative to make sense we must see more than she, must interpret the incidents she reports in a way different from hers. To the end, despite a good bit of evidence that should call her basic outlook into question, she remains what she was at the beginning;

namely, an optimist and a meliorist. To the degree that she is un-
changed by her experiences there is thus never any *Bildung* in the
part of the novel that she calls "my portion of these pages" (p. 17)
and that appears, at first glance, as akin to the *Bildungsroman.*

But if her narrative is not an autobiography, which she insists
it is not ("as if this . . . were the narrative of *my* life" [p. 27]),
why is she writing the story in which she is so heavily involved?
Who assigned her the task? Somehow she is "obliged to write"
(p. 27) this story ostensibly about others, but it ends up being
mainly "my story" (p. 729) for the benefit of "any one who may
read what I write" (p. 102), some "unknown friend" (p. 767).
Moreover, how does she know that her narrative is only a "portion" of these pages?[9] To write half of a book of which she
apparently recognizes the other half to have been written by an
omniscient narrator is tantamount to admitting her own fiction-
ality.

And such is precisely the case. Esther Summerson is not only
the ingenue of her narrative but also the novelist of her story. On
several occasions she reveals herself as a conscious artist carefully
constructing what she writes. About a certain incident she says:
"What more the letters told me, needs not to be repeated here. It
has its own times and places in my story" (p. 453). In similar
manner she says: "I must write" (p. 378), "I will not dwell"
(p. 703), "I proceed to other passages of my narrative" (p. 714),
"I may at once finish what I know of his history" (p. 729). Only a
conscientious craftsman would be at such pains to shape this
account. Made constantly aware of the narrator at work on her
narrative, we are unable to separate the teller from the tale. The
dancer and the dance, to paraphrase Yeats, blend into pure
artifice.

Where Esther's narrative is a personal fiction, the nameless
narrator's is an impersonal one. As W. J. Harvey observes, "The
general impression is of a vast, collective choric voice brilliantly
mimicking the varied life it describes."[10] And even though Esther
does not appear in the nameless narrator's part of the book, her

narrative is dependent upon his, is a "portion" of that chorus, and
is assimilated into it as another voice. Her narrative is therefore
but another document in the whole array of documents woven to
form the text of *Bleak House.*

The novel has been called "a document about the interpretation of documents."[11] I would argue that the profusion of documents attests to the novel's insistence upon its own textuality, its
status as a fiction and an artifice, in sum, a metafiction like
Carlyle's *Sartor Resartus.* From the beginning *Bleak House*
shows itself as a kind of theatrical world where the drama is
enacted in accordance with various scripts, references to which
are scattered throughout the novel.[12]

The celebrated opening of chapter 1 reads like the directions
for a stage setting for a play:

> London. Michaelmas Term lately over, and the Lord Chan-
> cellor sitting in Lincoln's Inn Hall. Implacable November
> weather. As much mud in the streets, as if the waters had but
> newly retired from the face of the earth. . . . Smoke lowering
> down from the chimney-pots, making a soft black drizzle, with
> flakes of soot in it as big as full-grown snow-flakes. . . . Dogs,
> undistinguishable in mire. Horses, scarcely better. . . . Foot
> passengers, jostling one another's umbrellas, in a general infec-
> tion of ill-temper, and losing their foot-hold at street-corners,
> where tens of thousands of other foot passengers have been
> slipping and sliding since the day broke. . . .
>
> Fog everywhere. Fog up the river. . . . Fog on the Essex
> marshes, fog on the Kentish heights. . . .
>
> Gas looming through the fog in divers places in the
> streets. . . . Most of the shops lighted two hours before their
> time. . . .

The curtain then rises and we are introduced to the High Court of
Chancery, where the costumed actors are "running their goat-hair
and horse-hair warded heads against walls of words, and making a
pretence of equity with serious faces, *as players might*" (p. 6,

italics added). Having enacted the drama of Jarndyce and Jarndyce
many times, the players find their roles by no means taxing. They
go through their business automatically. Mr. Tangle has played his
part for so long that "he is famous for it," and his eighteen
associates, "each armed with a little summary of eighteen hundred sheets, bob up like eighteen hammers in a piano-forte, make
eighteen bows, and drop into their eighteen places" (p. 9). In the
Court of Chancery Esther finds "no reality in the whole scene"
(p. 308).

Cursory deliberations out of the way, the Chancellor exits,
and the curtain closes briefly so "that we may pass from the one
scene to the other," to the world of fashion, where the chief
players are Sir Leicester and Lady Dedlock. Like the actors in the
Court of Chancery those in the world of fashion "have played at
strange games" (p. 10). "It is not a large world" in comparison
"to this world of ours" (p. 11), says the nameless narrator-play-
wright, as in a moment of parabasis he turns to address his audience. It is played out in a succession of lunches, dinners, balls,
"and other melancholy pageants" (p. 500). Yet the persons who
visit the Dedlocks in London or in Lincolnshire

> are the great actors for whom the stage is reserved. A People
> there are, no doubt—a certain large number of supernumeraries,
> who are to be occasionally addressed, and relied upon for
> shouts and choruses, as on the theatrical stage; but [they], their
> followers . . . and assigns, are the born first-actors, managers,
> and leaders, and no others can appear upon the scene for ever
> and ever. (p. 146)

From the scenes of law and fashion the rest of the drama of *Bleak
House* is to be enacted.

Nearly all the actors in the drama are aware of their status as
dramatis personae and the illusory nature of their theatrical en-
deavors. Miss Flite, the same as many of the characters involved
in Chancery suits, fully realizes that she is condemned to play a

part in a play that, for her at any rate, never ends, that she will "be always in expectation of what never comes," the famous "Judgement" of her case (p. 440). Richard Carstone is aware of his Don Quixote role, of "fighting with shadows and being defeated by them" (p. 489). Snagsby "is doubtful of his being awake and out—doubtful of the reality of the streets through which he goes—doubtful of the reality of the moon" (p. 284). And even Esther, who most of the time seems to have such a firm grip on what she perceives as reality, even she is not sure, during the search for her mother, that she is "not in a dream" (p. 676) or "that the unreal things were more substantial than the real" (p. 13). The sense of unreality—of make-believe, illusion, and theatricality—is heightened by the numerous disguises in which characters (for example, Lady Dedlock, Hortense, and Jenny) assume the dress of others or (like Esther's aunt and Captain Hawdon) assume different names and identities.

The list of aliases or number of roles that the actors play is very large, almost requiring a playbill for the reader-spectator. Captain Hawdon is also Nemo or Nimrod; Gridley is known as "the man from Shropshire"; Bartholomew Smallwood is called Small and Chick Weed; Tony Jobling assumes the alias of Mr. Weevle; Caroline Jellyby is known as Caddy, her brother as Peepy; George Rouncewell is called Trooper George, Old William Tell, and Old Shaw, the Life Guardsman; Jo is called Toughy or the Tough Subject; Mr. Bagnet is given the sobriquet Lignum Vitae; Mr. Kenge is Conversation Kenge; Ada and Richard are "Wards in Jarnydyce" and she is referred to by Esther only as "my darling"; Esther herself is called Old Woman, Cobweb, Mrs. Shipton, Mother Hubbard, Dame Durden, and Fitz-Jarndyce; the Snagsby's maid Augusta is nicknamed Guster; Krook calls himself Lord Chancellor; Esther's maid Charlotte is nicknamed Charley. With these numerous aliases and disguises it is no wonder that characters like Jo can say of Hortense disguised as Lady Dedlock, "It is her and it an't her" (p. 282); or that Mr. Jarndyce can say to George, "You talk of yourself as if you were somebody else!"

(p. 619); or that Sir Leicester can say to George, "You are another self to me" (p. 697).

The role that Lady Dedlock plays is that of the proud ennuyée, characterized by "an exhausted composure, a worn-out placidity, an equanimity of fatigue not to be ruffled by interest or satisfaction" (p. 13). Her pose is constant: she is "always the same exhausted deity" (p. 150). Yet "underneath that mask," she tells Esther, there is "the reality" of her suffering (p. 452). Few penetrate the disguise to see, as Tulkinghorn does, that "she has been acting a part" (p. 579); for "so long accustomed to suppress emotion, and keep down reality" (p. 663), she plays it perfectly.

Her husband assumes a complementary role, although there is less beneath the mask. He is "that effigy and figure-head of a baronet" (p. 220), always addressed by Bucket (as if reading from a program listing the cast of characters) as "Sir Leicester Dedlock, Baronet." Proud of his ancient name and exalted position, he loves the role of grand seigneur and "supposes all his dependents to be utterly bereft of individual characters, intentions, or opinions, and is persuaded that he was born to supersede the necessity of their having any" (p. 220).

Tulkinghorn, in his own quiet but mysterious way, is among the most theatrical of characters in *Bleak House*. Deliberately old-fashioned in dress, wearing knee breeches tied with ribbons and gaiters, he plays the role of "the steward of the legal mysteries, the butler of the legal cellar" (p. 14), at fashionable Chesney Wold, where he is "so oddly out of place, and yet so perfectly at home" (p. 150). He is "mute, close, irresponsive" (p. 14) with "a countenance as imperturbable as Death" (p. 429). He has no pity or anger and is "indifferent to everything but his calling," which is "the acquisition of secrets, and the holding possession of such power as they give him" (p. 451). Having gained "mastery" of this role (p. 503), he does not vary his repertory. As the nameless narrator says, "his own unchanging character" is the part "he can act" with perfection (p. 579).

Esther's role is also an unvarying one. It is that of the modest, meek, loyal, and loving young woman who enjoys being cast in the character of an elderly housekeeper. She describes herself as "a methodical, old-maidish sort of foolish little person" (p. 85) who willingly accepts being called Little Old Woman, Mother Hubbard, Dame Durden, "and so many names of that sort, that [her] own name soon became quite lost among them" (p. 90). She is the keeper of the keys, which are evidently pure stage properties because she never seems to unlock anything.

Of the lesser characters Skimpole is adept in the role of the "mere child" cheerfully refusing responsibility as "a thing that has always been above me–or below me" (p. 727). George Rouncwell is Trooper George who never relaxes his military bearing and rides "with imaginary clank and jingle of accoutrements" (p. 748). Bagnet likewise maintains his military role, constantly saying that "discipline must be maintained." Mr. Jellyby plays the part that cannot be described "better than by saying that he is the husband of Mrs. Jellyby" (p. 35). Mr. Quale is the "trainbearer and organ-blower to a whole procession" of other dramatis personae (p. 183). Mr. Turveydrop is "not like anything in the world but a model of Deportment" (p. 171), who acts the role of Regency dandy "like the second gentleman in Europe" (p. 292). Bucket has perfected the role of detective as he sneaks furtively about, seeming "in some undefinable manner to lurk and lounge" and pretending "to have a fixed purpose in his mind of going straight ahead, [then] wheels off, sharply, at the very last moment" (p. 277). Mr. Kenge, the lawyer, who in court is "truly eloquent" (p. 26), has "formed himself on the model of a great lord who was his client" (p. 23). Guppy, who "plays the deepest games of chess without any adversary" (p. 244), constantly rehearses the role of lawyer, sometimes haranguing his friend Tony as "gentlemen of the jury" (p. 251) and getting himself into "a state little short of forensic lunacy" (p. 495). Young Smallwood aims to emulate Guppy and "founds himself entirely on him" (p. 245). The French maid Hortense has modeled herself on the villains of melodrama; Chadband has elected to play the part of "orator."

Though many of these characters have freely chosen the

parts they play, others have had roles imposed upon them. Richard acts in a way "foreign to [his] nature" (p. 462), having been changed by his involvement in litigation (p. 464). Lady Dedlock initially believes that she manages others, whereas in fact "deferential people . . . manage her . . . , lead her" (p. 14). Ultimately she discovers that she must play a role as Tulkinghorn directs "on this gaudy platform, on which [her] miserable deception has been so long acted" (p. 512). In the same fashion George believes that he too must act as directed by Tulkinghorn, who, he says, "has got a power over me" and "keeps me on a constant see-saw" (p. 566).

Other characters seem to be little more than puppets or ventriloquists' dummies. Mr. Jellyby, controlled by his wife, never speaks but seems as if he would: he "several times opened his mouth . . . , as if he had something on his mind; but had always shut it again, . . . without saying anything" (p. 41). Mr. Pardiggle is like Mr. Jellyby; he is, says his wife, "under my direction" (p. 95). Snagsby is also ruled by his wife, who "manages the money, reproaches the Tax-gatherers, appoints the times and places of devotion on Sundays, [and] licenses Mr. Snagsby's entertainments" (p. 118). Though he and his wife are "one voice," that voice appears "to proceed from Mrs. Snagsby alone" (p. 117). Bagnet too has little voice save that given to him by his wife, whom he continually urges to tell what his opinion on a given subject might be. Without her, he, like a mannequin, cannot speak: "If my old girl had been here," he says, "I'd have told him!" (p. 426). Smallwood is like a puppet, which must be continually "shaken up," or a mechanical doll, which "having run down" must be wound up (p. 492). Rosa, who is being trained by Lady Dedlock, is referred to as "this doll, this puppet" (p. 143).

Esther conceives of herself in doll-like terms, even calling herself a "little person" (p. 85). Significantly, her first companion is a doll, and appropriately she is set up in the end by Mr. Jarndyce in a miniaturized Bleak House, with, as she says, "doll's rooms" suited to "*my* little tastes and fancies, *my* little methods and inventions" (p. 751). The "mere child" Skimpole would, says Mr. Jarndyce, also be suited to "a habitable doll's house," in which all a boy's desires would be fulfilled by someone else (p. 75). It is as though such characters possessed no life of their own but were dependent on someone or something to get them through their assigned parts.

Then there are persons like John Jarndyce, who, as guardian to Esther, Richard, and Ada, is constantly hovering in the background—and sometimes in the foreground—to guide them. In addition he is the benefactor to, among others, Miss Flite, Skimpole, and the Coavinses. He knows what others feel when they do not know it themselves. He "penetrated [Woodcourt's] secret when Dame Durden was blind to it" (p. 752). He arranges Esther's life almost from the beginning down to the point when she marries Woodcourt, presenting her, without any consultation about her wishes, a new Bleak House of which she is to be the mistress. Mainly he works his manipulations in silence and in secret, gaining knowledge of others without imparting information about himself. "I have long been in Allan Woodcourt's confidence," he says, "although he was not . . . in mine" (p. 752). Esther does not know till she is nineteen years old that he has been her benefactor for a long time.

Another "guardian"—guardian of the peace, as it were—is Bucket, who is "impossible to be evaded or declined" (p. 316). A shadowy presence, he is, says Jo, "in all manner of places, all at wunst" (p. 55) and further, again according to Jo, not only "everywhere" but "cognisant of everything" (p. 563). He keeps secret documents "in his book of Fate" (p. 629), the contents of which would incriminate almost everyone if they were revealed.

The notion of fate or of some superior power capable of appropriating the most trivial details and controlling their lives is uppermost in the minds of many of the characters of *Bleak House,* especially the suitors in Chancery, making them feel like puppets.[13] "There's a cruel attraction in the place," says Miss Flite. "You *can't* leave it" (p. 440). Gridley is, by his own account,

undone by "the system" (p. 193); nonetheless, he feels power-
less to abandon his insane fight against it. Richard Carstone is
the major example of the fatal attraction of Chancery. With him
as with the others, litigation becomes a monomania, "the object
of [his] life" (p. 464), which he feels "condemned" to pursue
(p. 288). By his own confession it leads him to madness as it had
Miss Flite and Gridley: "I can't help it now, and can't be sane"
(p. 546), because "I [am caught in] the net in which my destiny
has worked me" (p. 609). Even those who refuse active participation in suits in Chancery are nevertheless drawn into them against
their wills. For John Jarndyce the case of Jarndyce and Jarndyce is
"the ill-fated cause" (p. 9), "the family curse," "the horrible
phantom that has haunted us so many years" (p. 302). "We can't
get out of the suit on any terms, for we are made parties to it, and
must be parties to it, whether we like it or not" (p. 89). Why this
should be so is inexplicable: "How mankind ever came to be
afflicted . . . , or for whose sins these young people ever fell into
a pit of it, I don't know: so it is" (p. 91).

The Old Testament belief that the sins of the fathers are
visited upon the children, as found in Numbers 14:18, echoes
throughout the novel and on several occasions is specifically al-
luded to. As a child, and perhaps even as an adult, Esther is made
to feel guilty and "degraded" because of some past unknown
crime. "Your mother, Esther, is your disgrace," her aunt tells her,
"and you were hers." "Pray daily that the sins of others be not
visited upon your head" (p. 19, repeated p. 453). This degrada-
tion, the cause of which Esther learns only much later, has its
ramifications in the lives of her aunt, Boythorn, and of course her
mother, Lady Dedlock. Her aunt breaks off her engagement to be
married to Boythorn and dies an embittered spirit because of it.
For Boythorn "that time has had its influence on all his later
life. . . . He has never since been what he might have been"
(p. 111). Lady Dedlock's subsequent life has been governed by
guilt and her fear of the discovery of it. "The dark road I have
trodden for so many years will end where it will," she says resign-

edly. "I follow it alone to the end, whatever the end may be. . . ;
while the road lasts, nothing turns me" (p. 451). In each life there
seems to be, as Snagsby several times remarks, "quite a Fate in it.
Quite a Fate" (p. 395). So many of the actors feel, as Skimpole
declares, that like puppets they "have no Will at all" (p. 385) and
that their lives are governed by scripts collected in something like
Bucket's "book of Fate" (p. 629).

As many commentators on *Bleak House* have observed, the
novel abounds in references to documents and writings of all
kinds. Ink flows profusely: from Guppy's having "inked himself
by accident" (p. 28) to Caddy's being in "a state of ink" (p. 38)
to Jo's "Inkwhich" (p. 200) to Esther's closing narrative
"penned" in ink (p. 727). Papers relating to Jarndyce and Jarndyce exist in the thousands, perhaps millions, "great heaps, and
piles, and bags and bags-full" (p. 308), and "everybody must
have copies, over and over again, of everything that has accumu-
lated about it" (p. 88). The case ends with the discovery of a new
document, a will, amidst Krook's hoard of documents and the
subsequent destruction of "immense masses of papers" (p. 759).
Everyone seems obsessed with documents: Gridley, Miss Flite,
Richard, even Krook, whose "monomania . . . [is] to think he is
possessed of documents" (p. 401), but who cannot read or write.
Kenge and Tulkinghorn are always surrounded by papers. Snagsby and Nemo copy them, as does the illiterate Krook. Letterwrit-
ing is a major enterprise in the novel. Mrs. Jellyby and Mrs.
Pardiggle spend all day every day on correspondence; the start of
the feud between Boythorn and Sir Leicester begins with a letter
and reply; Mr. Jarndyce assumes responsibility for Esther because
of a letter from her aunt; Jarndyce proposes marriage to Esther not
orally but by means of a letter; Tulkinghorn drafts "mysterious
instructions" (p. 120); Lady Dedlock's letters to Captain Hawdon
are responsible for her undoing; Tulkinghorn discovers Lady Dedlock's secret by matching the handwriting on a letter in George's
possession to the documents copied by Nemo; Hortense's letters
of accusation of Lady Dedlock fall about "like a shower of lady-

birds" (pp. 650–51); Lady Dedlock's last words are letters. In
short, letters and documents of all sorts are basic to the plot and
texture of the novel.

They are important because the actors view them as scripts
authorizing their performances on the stage of *Bleak House*. Re-
ceiving Mr. Jarndyce's letter of proposal, Esther learned it "by
heart" and "repeated its contents" immediately (p. 734) and then
later "repeated every word of the letter twice over" (p. 750).
Then comes Woodcourt's proposal, which was "an unforeseen
page in my life" (p. 731). In his interview with Lady Dedlock,
Guppy reads, with difficulty, from a script that he himself has
prepared (pp. 360–61). In the beginning Caddy Jellyby "can't do
anything hardly, except write" at her mother's direction (p. 44),
but as it turns out, this has been valuable experience because her
husband, Prince Turveydrop, is very bad at writing and Caddy
must "write letters enough for both" (p. 177). Lady Dedlock is
forced into the position where, she says to Tulkinghorn, "I will
write anything . . . that you will dictate" (p. 509). As for the
lawyer himself, his destiny is not in the stars but "written in other
characters nearer to hand" (p. 507). At Richard's start of yet
another career John Jarndyce is hopeful that there has been "a new
page turned for you to write your lives in" (p. 303), but this new
page turns out to be one from "dusty bundles of papers which
seemed . . . like dusty mirrors reflecting his own mind" (p. 611).
Even Jo, who knows so little of the written word, wants spelled
out "wery large so that any one could see it anywheres" his regret
at giving the fever to Esther (p. 570). In the world of the novel a
thing apparently takes on reality in the minds of the actors only
when it is written. Thus the doll's house in Yorkshire becomes a
new Bleak House when it is re-presented verbally, that is, when it
has "written over it, BLEAK HOUSE" (p. 751). Bucket alone of
all the actors is averse to writing, being "no great scribe" because
to him the written word is "too artless and direct a way of doing
delicate business" (p. 629). Which is to say, faced with a script he

feels constrained by it. And yet even he is governed by one: "I say what I must say," he admits, "and no more" (p. 638).

Hovering above the stage on which the play is enacted is the author who in fact has written "the book of Fate," *Bleak House,* from which the actors are assigned their parts. For the most part he is content to be transcendent, to be a spectator looking down on his creation. Occasionally, however, he descends onto the stage, becomes immanent in his work, and lets the audience witness him among the players. We see him in the third-person narrative when he breaks into the action to address his players or, even, his audience. "Do you hear, Jo?" (p. 238). "Young man of the name of Guppy" (p. 361). "Look at a millstone, Mr. George, for some change in its expression, and you will find it quite as soon as in the face of Mr. Tulkinghorn" (p. 429). These are among the apostrophes to his characters. And among the direct addresses to his audience there is the famous parabasis following the death of Jo:

> Dead, your Majesty. Dead, my lords and gentlemen. Dead,
> Right Reverends and Wrong Reverends of every order. Dead,
> men and women, born with Heavenly compassion in your
> hearts. And dying thus around us every day. (p. 572)

There are also remarks made to "Your Highness" (pp. 11, 403), whose identity is never revealed, remarks that seem to be made solely for the purpose of the author's intrusion into the narrative.

We can never know who "Your Highness" is any more than we can identify in the fictional world who assigned Esther to write "my portion of these pages" or who might be the "unknown friend to whom I write" and from whom she will part "not without much dear remembrance" (even though she does not know him or her) (p. 767). We shall never know because Dickens did not intend for us to know. What he did intend was for us to recognize the presence of the author in his work, to see the stage

manager controlling the action and commenting on it. Even in
Esther's narrative we catch a glimpse of him from time to time.
We see him, for example, behind Esther's remarks in this collo-
quy with Miss Flite:

> "My dear," said she, . . . "my brave physician ought to
> have a Title bestowed upon him. And no doubt he will. You are
> of that opinion?" . . .
>
> I said it was not the custom in England to confer titles on
> men distinguished by peaceful services, however good and
> great; unless occasionally, when they consisted of the accumula-
> tion of some very large amount of money.
>
> "Why good gracious," said Miss Flite, "how can you say
> that? Surely you know . . . that all the greatest ornaments of
> England in knowledge, imagination, active humanity, and im-
> provement of every sort, are added to its nobility! . . . *You*
> must be rambling a little now . . . if you don't know that this is
> the great reason why titles will always last in the land!"
>
> I am afraid she believed what she said; for there were
> moments when she was very mad indeed. (pp. 442–43)

This is not *Esther* speaking, as anyone who has read thus far in the
novel can easily discern. This kind of irony is foreign to her
nature, and Dickens, who was perfectly capable of controlling the
tone of his characters' remarks, knew it. This is, as Browning
might have said, "Charles Dickens *loquitur.*" His aim is to break
the fictional illusion, to step onto the stage, to comment, and in
effect, to say: "This is not life enacted here. It is art, not a
representation but a re-presentation of life, and I am the artist."

The authorial voice is of course discoverable in many other
of Dickens's works. *Bleak House* is different from his earlier
novels, however, in that in addition to his voice there is the
author's presence hovering over the proceedings. It is the kind of
suspended presence that in 1849 he envisioned for himself in the
magazine he wished to edit. It was to be "a certain SHADOW,
which may go into any place, . . . and be . . . cognisant of ev-

erything, . . . a kind of semi-omniscient, omnipresent, intangible creature." In brief, this authorial "shadow" was to be "an odd, unsubstantial, whimsical, new thing: a sort of previously unthought-of Power going about . . . everyone's inseparable companion."[14] When *Household Words* was in fact launched in 1850, Dickens insisted on the principle of anonymity, all the articles being unsigned; on the masthead, however, Dickens was identified as its "Conductor," and across the top of each page there were printed the words "Conducted by Charles Dickens." It was, as Douglas Jerrold remarked, "*mono*nymous throughout."[15]

The egotistical sublime was a very strong component of Dickens's nature. In *Bleak House,* however, he managed sufficiently to subdue this aspect of his personality to the negatively capable and to merge with it to the point where, like the Christian God, he could be both immanent and transcendent. Looking down on his creation he entertains and tolerates the rival views—of order and of chaos, of being and of becoming—expressed by his dual narrators.[16] Entering into his fictive world he, not unlike Thackeray's Manager of the Performance, sympathizes with the physical and moral plight of his characters. He is a kind of presiding "shadow," who is both optimistic and pessimistic, who accepts free will as well as determinism, and who, with a kind of Nietzschean gaiety, witnesses the world being constantly created and de-created, formed in order to be transformed. The universe he presents is one where meaning is neither fixed nor absent but always becoming. In sum, Dickens shows himself in *Bleak House* as a tough-minded romantic ironist engaged in the serious business of metaphysical, aesthetic, and ethical play. The nimbleness and agility of "mononymity" manifested here he would never quite attain elsewhere.

6

"THE OLD ORDER CHANGETH"
Idylls of the King

As an adherent of the doctrine of becoming, Tennyson is as full of contradiction and paradox as the Bible. "All truth is change," he says in an early poem, "for nothing is, but all is made."[1] And embracing this Heraclitean concept, he writes poems of contrasting and discrepant views expressive of his understanding that cosmos arises from chaos and sinks into chaos again. "Nothing Will Die" is matched in the *Poems, Chiefly Lyrical* (1830) by "All Things Will Die." "Tithonus," about the desire for dissolution, was composed as a companion to "Ulysses," "about the need of going forward and braving the struggle of life" (Ricks, p. 560). Such contradictions are, however, generally held beneath the surface in *In Memoriam* (1850), which gives an apocalyptic view of human perfection resulting from physical and spiritual evolution. Yet, significantly, upon completing it Tennyson stated that his poem was far more optimistic about the fate of humankind than he was. "It's too hopeful, this poem, more than I am myself," he said. "I think of adding another to it, a speculative one, . . . showing that all the arguments are about as good on one side as the other, and thus throw man back more on the primitive impulses and feelings" (Ricks, pp. 859–60). *Idylls of the King* fits this description beautifully, for it presents a narrative fully informed by the poet's concept of becoming.

94

At the close of the poem, as the light fades following the Great Battle in the West, King Arthur in his dying moments laments, "[A]ll my realm / Reels back into the beast, and is no more." The land where he felled the forest and which he cleared of beast and pagan reverts to the condition in which the King originally found it. What has caused the collapse of Camelot and all the spiritual ideals to which its maker aspired? This has been a subject of debate in Tennyson studies over the past forty years. On one side are those who hold the traditional view that "the one sin [of Lancelot and Guinevere] determines the calamity of the kingdom"; on the other side, those who maintain that different destructive forces are responsible for the downfall and that "the sin of Guinevere is merely the symbol and not the source of the decline of the Round Table."[2] In my opinion both views, though contradictory, are tenable and were, in fact, held by the poet himself.

Of the completed *Idylls* Tennyson commented: "The whole . . . is the dream of man coming into practical life and ruined by one sin" (Ricks, p. 1463). And of the individual idylls he said, for example, of "Lancelot and Elaine" that here "the tenderest of all natures sinks under the blight" (Ricks, p. 1621), and of "The Last Tournament" that "the great sin of Lancelot was sapping the Round Table" (Ricks, p. 1710n). Speaking of "The Holy Grail" he claimed, "I have expressed there my strong feeling as to the Reality of the Unseen" (Ricks, p. 1661). Yet in his notes to this idyll the poet undermined this "Reality" by saying of the Grail quest, "It was a time of storm when men could imagine miracles, and so storm is emphasized" (Ricks, p. 1676n), and by saying of Bors's vision of the Grail, "It might have been a meteor" (Ricks, p. 1680n). Of Merlin's vision of heavenly signs in "Gareth and Lynette" (ll. 249–50), the poet notes that it was "Refraction by mirage" (Ricks, p. 1490n). Further, when his friend J. T. Knowles wrote a letter to the *Spectator* (1 January 1870) praising the "realism" of the *Idylls* that allows "accounting naturally for all the supernatural adventures and beliefs recorded in the story itself," Tennyson acknowledged that Knowles's was *"the best, and indeed . . . the only true, critique of the Idylls."*[3]

Tennyson was usually pleased to have his readers recognize a higher, allegorical significance in the *Idylls,* but he disliked being pinned down as to his exact meaning. "They are right, and they are not right," he said of some interpreters of his poem. As for certain details, "They mean that and they do not. . . . I hate to be tied down to say, *'This* means *that'*. . ." (Ricks, p. 1463). His exegetes have, he maintained, "taken my hobby, and ridden it too hard, and have explained some things too allegorically, although there is an allegorical or perhaps rather a parabolic drift in the poem" (Ricks, p. 1463). "Poetry is," he held, "like shot-silk with many glancing colours. Every reader must find his own interpretation according to his ability, and according to his sympathy with the poet" (Ricks, p. 1463).

We seem to have Tennyson's own warrant, then, for at least two interpretations of the *Idylls*—one that, as we have remarked, the poet authorized, an idealist reading; and one of which he was more than half conscious but refrained from sanctioning explicitly, namely, a realistic or naturalistic reading. Such contradictory views of his poem, the author realized, were inherent in his treatment of the Arthurian material, the nature of which he dealt with, in barely disguised fashion, in the first of the idylls that he wrote with the specific intention of forming a cycle of poems, the one finally called "Merlin and Vivien." Tennyson had been fascinated by the story of Arthur since early youth: "The vision of an ideal Arthur as I have drawn him . . . had come upon me when, little more than a boy, I first lighted upon Malory" (Ricks, p. 1464). Yet when he looked into other Arthurian sources, he discovered a less than "ideal Arthur." "On Malory, on Layamon's *Brut,* on Lady Charlotte Guest's translation of the *Mabinogion,* on the old Chronicles, on French Romance, on Celtic folklore, and largely on his own imagination, my father founded his epic," Hallam Tennyson noted (Ricks, p. 1460). Yet, as Swinburne with his usual keenness observed, the materials were incongruous and "radically incapable of combination or coherence. Between the various Arthurs of different national legends there is little more in common than the name. It is essentially impossible to construct a human figure by the process of selection from the incompatible types of irreconcilable ideals."[4] Tennyson himself admitted, "How much of history we have in the story of Arthur is doubtful. Let not my readers press too hardly on details whether for history or for allegory" (Ricks, p. 1469). To get at the real Arthur, then, meant dealing with a wealth of sources that might or might not yield the "ideal" for which the poet was searching.

In a section of "Merlin and Vivien" that Tennyson noted was not in any of his sources (Ricks, p. 1611n), the poet tells of a book that had belonged to a wise man who, penetrating the wall dividing spirit and matter, set down, with "an inky cloud," what "charms" he had discovered (ll. 616–48). Now in the hands of Merlin, the book consists of twenty pages, each containing in the middle a microscopic text "writ in a language that had long gone by" (l. 672). Surrounding the text are margins "scribbled, crost, and crammed / With comment, densest condensation, hard / To mind and eye" (ll. 675–77). No one can read the text, and only Merlin can read the comment. The ur-text, in other words, is quite irrecoverable. Only the commentary—the tradition, as it were—can be reclaimed, but that by one man alone, the mage with whom the poet obviously identifies. From the matter of history and earliest legend it is impossible to penetrate the "inky cloud" to get at the real Arthur. What the "comment"—the many incongruous retellings of the Arthurian story—provides is only a shadowy figure about whom the most contradictory attributes are said to be true. There may be, as Tennyson held, "no grander subject in the world than King Arthur" (Ricks, p. 1464), but for the poet who undertakes a long poem based on it there is always the possibility of being "charmed" by it into inactivity, an inability to complete his project, as Merlin was charmed by Vivien and so "lost to life and use and name and fame" (l. 968).

Aware then, however faintly, of incompatible sources offer-

ing a hero of irreconcilable qualities, Tennyson proceeded to draw
the antitypes of "The True and the False" (as his first two idylls
were called when set up in a trial edition in 1857) revolving
around his central figure. From the beginning Tennyson held a
double focus on his idylls, providing, as David Shaw remarks, an
"anatomy of the saint and soldier, the skeptic and the dupe, the
sensualist and the stoic."[5] His poem, said the poet in the epilogue
"To the Queen," was an "old imperfect tale / New-old, and shad-
owing Sense at war with Soul." If his audience wished to stress
sensuality as the "one sin" ruining "the dream," they apparently
had the sanction of the poet himself, who seemed to revise and
expand the *Idylls* to relate all manifestations of the collapse of
Camelot to Guinevere's infidelity.[6]

   According to this reading, in the first idyll, "The Coming of
Arthur," a veil of lustre is thrown over Arthur's origin, his authority hidden in mystery. However, his claim to kingship is con-
firmed by his subsequent deeds, his knights' faith in him, Belli-
cent's belief in his supernatural birth, Leodogran's dream of his
legitimacy, and Merlin's claim that "from the great deep to the
great deep he goes" (CA, l. 410; LT, l. 133; PA, l. 445), meaning
that he will never die but will come again. As soul or spirit,
Arthur seeks in his marriage to Guinevere a means of embodiment
in order to achieve the wholeness of what Tennyson called "the
character of Christ, that union of man and woman, strength and
sweetness" (Ricks, p. 1687). The King joined to his Queen and
surrounded by knights sworn to reverence him and do his bidding,
this Maytime at Camelot is a season of unity and hope.

   "Gareth and Lynette" represents, in the words of the poet's
wife, "the golden time of Arthur's court" (Ricks, p. 1484), characterized by perfect courage, perfect faith, perfect love. Gareth is
the type of youthful, enthusiastic loyalty and hardihood, gladly
willing to undertake any chore, no matter how lowly or igno-
minious, in the service of the King. In aid of virtue he fights and
overcomes the allegorical figures of the day and night (life and
death), unmasks the last (which is shown to be a mere boy), and

delivers the captive spirit from the enthrallments of the flesh in the
Castle Perilous. By the time of the third and fourth idylls—"The
Marriage of Geraint" and "Geraint and Enid"—the infection of
disloyalty has set in, breeding distrust as the rumor of Guinevere's
unfaithfulness spreads out. "The sin of Lancelot and Guinevere
begins to breed, even among those who would 'rather die than
doubt,' despair and want of trust in God and man," Hallam Tennyson commented (Ricks, p. 1551). Camelot has been shown to
be governed by the interacting ideals of Christian duty, courtly
love, and chivalric valor, for the knights of the Round Table have
sworn to "utter hardihood, utter gentleness, / . . . utter faithfulness in love, / And uttermost obedience to the King" (GL,
ll. 542–44). Any chink in the towering city, any false or discordant note in this edifice built to music (GL, ll. 272–73), can cause
the collapse of the whole. In time Geraint recognizes Enid's spot-
less innocence and is reclaimed from distrust and death by it and
the King's healing influence. The reformation of Edryn further
illustrates the Round Table in its early purity, when love and
loyalty are rewarded.

    In "Balin and Balan" rumor has become slander with the
introduction of Vivien, who as the personification of lust is, in
Hallam Tennyson's words, "the evil genius of the Round
Table . . . who in her lustfulness of the flesh could not believe in
anything either good or great" (Ricks, p. 1593). Language has
become debased, religion (in the observances of Pellam) turned to
superstitution, obligation deformed to selfishness. "Loyal natures
are wrought to anger and madness against the world," Tennyson
said in reference to this idyll (Ricks, p. 1576), as the sin of
Lancelot and Guinevere becomes more widely known. In "Merlin
and Vivien," Tennyson commented, "Some even among the
highest intellects become the slaves of the evil which is at first
half disdained" (Ricks, p. 1595). The flesh, in the figure of Vivien, corrupts and immobilizes the intellect, Merlin, who, though
recognizing true spirituality, is yet not endowed with its moral
power, a quality that is shown when Arthur withstands Vivien's

seductive moves. Intellect thus victimized, the soul is robbed of its shrewdest ally. Even though the corrosive influence of Guinevere's infidelity is thus demonstrated, Camelot is not yet totally perverted. The knights resist Vivien's blandishments, because nothing external, as it turns out, can seriously threaten the city, the corruption lying within.

In "Lancelot and Elaine" the lily maid's first love is contrasted with the Queen's jealousy and guilty passion. Arthur's influence declines and Gawain, the type of man indifferent to all save pleasure, trifles with the King's orders. Lancelot's suffering and remorse prepare the way for the thirst for expiation in "The Holy Grail," in which the characters display a yearning for wonders and a mystic passion for the unseen at the expense of practical duty and social responsibility. Although all the knights, except Gawain, who go on the journey find some kind of spiritual enrichment, the quest for the holy cup of healing in fact maims Arthur's order. Guinevere is entirely correct when she says to the departing knights, "This madness has come on us for our sins" (1. 357).

In "Pelleas and Ettarre," in the poet's opinion "almost the saddest of the Idylls" (Ricks, p. 1687), the victory of lust is complete. With the growth of sensual anarchy, Pelleas, a type of youthful and enthusiastic purity like Gareth, is betrayed by a member of the Round Table. Deceived by Gawain and having no Enid to support him, the raw, idealistic youth turns, in reaction and desperation, into the Red Knight, the wild antithesis to Arthur, and establishes the Round Table in the North, representing the opposite of all that for which Camelot stands. Whereas in this idyll the ideal of courtly love fails, leaving innocence impotent, in "The Last Tournament" the whole notion of love, chastity, and fidelity is depraved. Using doubt as a convenience, Tristram assumes license in all things. Because the idealism of Camelot was betrayed, he turns to "nature," the world of animal lust, for his sanction. "Crown'd warrant had we for our crowning sin" (1. 572), he tells his mistress Isolt, while her husband, Mark, the type of undisciplined and unprincipled intelligence, cleaves him through the brain. Only Dagonet, the fool, upholds the King.

In "Guinevere," which has been called "the central idyll in terms of moral design,"[7] evil has almost conquered, while one of those persons whose actions permitted evil to enter recognizes the extent of her misconduct. Modred, the type of beastly, shadowy malignity and antagonist of all good in Camelot, has taken over the city. Guinevere, now in refuge, is vaguely aware of her serious offense; only when faced by Arthur himself does she become fully conscious of her sin. The downfall of the kingdom has come about "all through thee" (l. 489), the King tells her, at the same time forgiving her. Now realizing that she was a traitor to love when her duty was to love the highest, she turns away from her passionate love for Lancelot to love for Arthur and hopes for reunion with her husband in heaven. Absolved of her sin, she sees the King as the embodiment of virtue and herself as seduced by "false voluptuous pride, that took / Full easily all impressions from below" (ll. 634–37). After repentence and years of good deeds and a pure life, she is redeemed.

"The Passing of Arthur" represents, said Tennyson, "the temporary triumph of evil, the confusion of moral order, closing in the Great Battle of the West" (Ricks, p. 1742). In this last idyll Arthur, like Christ in the final hours, experiences forsaken suffering and a feeling of betrayed innocence. Spirit seems to fail utterly and virtue to pass entirely. Yet in the end, when the arm catches the sword Excalibur and the barge bearing the three Queens comes to fetch him to the island-valley of Avilion, spirit triumphs over flesh. Rising from the doubt of "My God, thou hast forgotten me in my death" to the affirmation of "Nay—God my Christ—I pass but shall not die" (ll. 27–28), and promising to come again, the King sails off into the distance while from the dawn echoes a great cry and the sun rises, hopefully, bringing a new year. "The purpose of the individual man may fail for a time," the poet observed of the close of his poem, "but his work cannot die" (Ricks, p. 1754n).

No doubt "the vision of an ideal Arthur" (Ricks, p. 1464) had inspired the poet. Ruminating on his subject, he had held that "'in short, God has not made since Adam was, the man more perfect than Arthur,' as an old writer says" (Ricks, p. 1469). Yet dealing with his diverse, incompatible sources offering an incoherent picture of his hero, Tennyson could not conceal from himself or his readers the irreconcilable elements lying at the heart of his story. In his own idealistic formulation of the legend certain discrepancies became immediately apparent. Why, for instance, in "Gareth and Lynette," in the springtime of Camelot, is Sir Kay so boorish?[8] Why does the illicit relationship between Lancelot and Guinevere begin apparently even before or possibly soon after her marriage to the King (MV, ll. 772–75)? Why, if Vivien is "the evil genius of the Round Table" personifying lust (Ricks, p. 1593), does Lancelot's adulterous affair with the Queen commence before Vivien appears? Why, more importantly, is Arthur so blind to the world around him, "against [his] own eye-witness fain [to] / Have all men true and leal, all women pure" (MV, ll. 791–92)? Such anomalies could not be explained away, and in order to deal with them, Tennyson had to look at his Arthur, at least his original conception of him, in a different, less idealistic way.

Of the *Idylls of the King* the poet's son noted that "the completed poem, regarded as a whole, gives his innermost being more fully, though not more truly, than *In Memoriam*" (Ricks, p. 1464). And of *In Memoriam* itself, as we have seen, the poet said that it was too hopeful and that he thought of adding another poem to it to show that the arguments were about as good on one side as the other. This is a characteristically Tennysonian way of proceeding, first asserting and then, in some fashion or other, undermining the assertion. Thus Arthur Hallam, who in *In Memoriam* represents the type of idealized manhood that posits the way to perfected humanity, is balanced by another Arthur, "the flower of kings" of Joseph of Exeter, the idealized type who witnesses the retrogression inevitably attendant upon progress. Where

Arthur Hallam appeared "ere the times were ripe" (*In Memoriam,*
epilogue, l. 139), the earth not yet ready to receive its saints; King
Arthur appears at the opportune time to demonstrate that the earth
will never be ready to receive them permanently. As a speaker in
another of Tennyson's poems says, it is a case of "Chaos, Cosmos! Cosmos, Chaos!"—of "Evolution ever climbing after some
ideal good, / And Reversion ever dragging Evolution in the mud"
("Locksley Hall Sixty Years After," ll. 127, 199–200).

   In the *Idylls* Arthur appears mysteriously, with the authority
of the spiritual deep or of legitimate succession—or without any
authority at all. Whatever his origin, he must impose his authority
by force, ridding the land of beast and pagan, felling the forest
and letting in the light, and subjecting his followers to his will. As
part of his plan for rule he has had erected the marvelous city of
Camelot, the objective embodiment of his will, always in process,
it being "built / To music, therefore never built at all, / And
therefore built for ever" (GL, ll. 272–74).[9] He then marries
Guinevere so that their union will be a model of love and marriage: "for saving I be joined / To her . . . I . . . cannot will my
will, nor work my work / Wholly, nor make myself in mine own
realm / Victor and lord" (CA, ll. 84–89). Further he binds his
knights "by so strait vows to his own self" that they assume "a
momentary likeness of the King" (CA, ll. 261, 270), and demands of them "utter hardihood, utter gentleness, / And, loving,
utter faithfulness in love, / And uttermost obedience to the King"
(GL, ll. 541–44). Asking them in effect to be little Arthurs, the
King imposes himself on them by robbing them of their own
wills. "The King will follow Christ, and we the King," they sing,
so that "Arthur and his knighthood for a space / Were all one
will" (CA, ll. 499, 514–15).

   As the epilogue explains, Arthur is "Ideal manhood closed in
real man." The knights of the Round Table, however, are not ideal
men, nor is Guinevere the ideal woman; and swearing to perfect
behavior is, of course, swearing to the impossible and thus provides the ground for guilt. Merlin, the highest intellect in Cam-

elot, makes this very clear to Gareth when he outlines what the King requires:

> Yet take thou heed of him, for, so thou pass
> Beneath this archway, then wilt thou become
> A thrall to his enchantments, for the King
> Will bind thee by such vows, as is a shame
> A man should not be bound by, yet the which
> No man can keep. (GL, ll. 263–68)

As we shall see, the knights' feeling of guilt, resulting from their inability to keep their vows, and their subsequent emotional dependency on someone or something to sustain selfhood are pervasive in the succeeding idylls.

The notion of role-playing—or the search for a stable identity or "name" to which the notion is closely allied—is an important theme in the *Idylls* almost from the beginning. Costumes and disguises figure prominently, as do verbal distortions and outright lies, the linguistic mask of thought. Correctly viewed from the idealist standpoint, all disguises, sartorial or linguistic, are reprehensible in that they misrepresent the truth, the thing itself. Even at the commencement of those ten idylls forming "The Round Table" disguise enters into the story of Arthur's kingdom and, paradoxically, is tolerated and encouraged by the King. Gareth dresses as a youth of low birth, serves as a kitchen-knave, and goes on a quest under the pretense that he is working his way up from the kitchen. "Let be my name until I make my name!" he says (GL, l. 562). Merlin views all this as misbehavior: Gareth has set about "to mock the King, / Who cannot brook the shadow of any lie." And Gareth himself is uneasy in this feigned role: "Our one white lie sits like a little ghost / Here on the threshold of our enterprise" (GL, ll. 286–87, 291–92). Yet Arthur, who is fully aware of the circumstances, acquiesces in the pretense first to Kay and then to Lynette. The reason for this, as Tennyson makes explicit later, is that the ideal is transcendent and can be even partially manifested or grasped only when brought down to earth, embodied in the imperfections of phenomenal reality. Arthur cannot, in other words, be effective, be other than a figure-head ideal, unless he descends from ethereal perfection into the falsities of matter. And if Arthur acts this way, how can his subjects be expected to do otherwise?

Geraint pretends that his lands are imperiled so that he can take his wife away from the corrupting influence of the Queen, about whom he has merely heard a rumor of misconduct. Falsely believing Enid unfaithful, he insists that she return to her earlier, pristine state and dress in the lowly costume in which he original-ly saw her, although he had previously aimed "to dress her beau-tifully and keep her true" (GE, l. 40). Eventually restored to physical and moral health by his wife, on whom he had become fully dependent, Geraint recovers his proper status in Camelot, forswears disguise, and relishes Enid clothed by the Queen "in apparel like the day" (GE, l. 947).

Balin is dependent upon Balan for his balance. Without his twin he believes, guiltily, "Too high this mount of Camelot for me" (BB, l. 221). As a prop for his identity he bears the Queen's crown-royal upon his shield, but when he discovers her false, he tramples the shield, mistakenly murders his brother, and dies. Before his death, however, he is persuaded that those who had told him tales about the Queen were liars and that "pure as our own true Mother is our Queen" (BB, l. 606), which means that he is as deluded in sanity as he was in madness. Although it is the purpose of the King to be a light unto his people—and indeed he is usually associated with images of blazing light—the fact re-mains, as the narrator says earlier, that men do but grope "through the feeble twilight of this world" forever "taking true for false, or false for true" (GE, ll. 4–5).

Merlin is the first to recognize that, however high the aspira-tions of the King for the inhabitants of the towering city of Cam-elot, the hopes can never be realized, that, in fact, they are the cause of their own undoing. Against all evidence of fallibility, the

King has persevered in his aim to make his subjects perfect. He has been unable to accommodate himself to the world in both deed and word, his "over-fineness not intelligible" (MV, ll. 791–94). Foreseeing the destruction of Camelot, Merlin has left the city in melancholy and distress, and looking for someone to sustain him, he turns to Vivien "and half believed her true" (MV, l. 398), in the end yielding to her wiles and becoming "lost to life and use and name and fame" (MV, l. 968).

"Lancelot and Elaine" returns to the theme of disguise when Lancelot enters the tournament unidentified. The knight worries about the pretext he must make to the King to do this, but Guinevere, no doubt rightly, argues that the King will allow the ruse because it is done for glory. "No keener hunter after glory breathes," she says. "He loves it in his knights more than himself: / They prove to him his work" (LE, ll. 155–57). Only in overcoming the not-self is the spiritual "I" realized. For this very reason Arthur has been "rapt in this fancy of his Table Round, / And swearing men to vows impossible" (LE, 129–30). To Guinevere as to others at court it is the King's unforgivable fault to be faultless. How is it possible to love an ideal, an abstraction, a remote heavenly presence? "For who loves me must have a touch of earth," she says not unreasonably, and therefore, turning to Lancelot, "I am yours" (LE, ll. 133, 134). The guilt engendered by their adulterous relationship is almost intolerable for her lover and leads to the next idyll in which the knights of the Round Table, all too conscious of their failure to live up to what they have sworn, seek to substitute allegiance to a higher cause for their vows to the King.

"The Holy Grail" shows the increasing impotence of Arthur's will and the appearance of other dominant wills. Even though earlier Arthur had been successful in the creation of knights "stampt with the image of the King" (HG, l. 27), the disaffection with Camelot is evident in the three preceding idylls. Then comes news of a *frisson nouveau* in the kingdom. In an erotic ecstasy a nun claims to have had a vision of the Holy Grail. When this

information is communicated to Galahad, he visits the nun, who
"laid her mind / On him, and he believed in her belief" (ll. 164–
65). Soon after, while Arthur is away, there arises a storm, and
what may be a burst of lightning sends blinding light into the hall
where the knights are assembled. They all believe that it is the Grail
appearing unto them, although no one seems to have seen it.
Percivale swears, *because he has not seen the Grail,* to ride in quest
of it, and in this vow he is followed by others, although earlier they
had sworn, "The King will follow Christ, and we the King" (CA,
l. 499). As happens with others who depart from Camelot, they are
left unsupported and become either lost or mad. Galahad attains the
vision, apparently because the nun had willed him to see it.
Percivale, too, claims to see it, because, he says, Galahad with his
eye "drew me, with power upon me, till I grew / One with him, to
believe as he believed" (ll. 486–87). Whether the others saw
anything is unclear. Arthur himself is suspicious of all the visions
save Galahad's, guardedly saying, "if indeed there came a sign
from heaven" (l. 869). He is fully cognizant of the meaning of this
exchange of their vows of allegiance from himself to a vision, and
he ends the idyll by saying that the questers should have followed
his example, postponing heavenly vision till earthly work be done.

As much in love with love as Elaine, who "lived in fantasy"
(LE, l. 27), Pelleas seeks a beloved who will be "my Queen, my
Guinevere" so that he can be "thine Arthur when we meet" (PE,
ll. 44–45). As it happens, Ettarre is false to him, and so is Gawain,
whom he sent to woo on his behalf. The untrue love and the untrue
knight's betrayal argue in his mind that "the King / Hath made us
fools and liars. O noble vows!"(PE, ll. 469–70). Because built
"too high," Camelot has turned into a "black nest of rats," and
Pelleas is left with "no name, no name" (ll. 543–44, 553). Totally
disillusioned with all that Arthur represents, Pelleas becomes the
Red Knight and establishes a Round Table in the North which is the
antithesis to Camelot and where men profess themselves no better
than they are.

Even though he remains nominally in Arthur's camp, Tristram

belongs emotionally and morally with Pelleas in the North. Admitting that he has broken his vows, he argues that they never should have been made in the first place. Arthur has been totally unrealistic all along. In demanding so much, he has planted the seed of failure: "The vow that binds too strictly snaps itself—/ . . . ay, being snapt— / We run more counter to the soul thereof / Than had we never sworn" (LT, ll. 652–55). Admittedly, in the beginning the vows, "the wholesome madness of an hour," served their use, for every knight believed himself capable of higher things than he had ever dreamed. But then disillusion set in, and the vows began to gall. Whence, the knights ask,

> Had Arthur right to bind them to himself?
> Dropt down from heaven? washed up from out the deep?
> They failed to trace him through the flesh and blood
> Of our old kings: whence then? a doubtful lord
> To bind them by inviolable vows,
> Which flesh and blood perforce would violate: . . .
>   we are not angels here
> Nor shall be . . . . (LT, ll. 679–84, 693–94)

Tristram is of course rationalizing and justifying his failure to perform as he had sworn, but the appositeness of his utterance is brought home by Dagonet, the fool, who, recalling Merlin's remarks about the stainless King, terms Arthur "my brother fool, the king of fools" who "conceits himself as God that he can make / Figs out of thistles, silk from bristles, milk / From burning spurge, honey from hornet-combs, / And men from beasts." The aim may be noble, but ultimately it is foolish. And so in half praise and half dispraise he apostrophizes Arthur: "Long live the king of fools!" (LT, ll. 354–58).

In the last idyll of "The Round Table" Arthur confronts Guinevere and rehearses his plans, now laid waste, for Camelot. He speaks to her not as an outraged husband but as an offended ruler. He had established his order of the Table Round "to serve as model for the mighty world," binding his knights by vows to reverence himself and aim for perfect conduct. He had married Guinevere so that she could feel his purpose and work his work. Now, she having "spoilt the purpose of [his] life," he has no desire to live (G, ll. 449–80). It is no wonder that she had always "thought him cold, / High, self-contained, and passionless" (G, ll. 402–3). For it is clear that he loved her not as a woman but as an idea, the model of an ideal queen, as he was the model of the ideal king.

In the final idyll Arthur in his last moments seems to understand where he had gone wrong. From the beginning he had but one goal in life: to establish a perfect kingdom, to make Camelot a New Jerusalem. But he had not taken into account the impregnable amorality of nature: "I perish by this people which I made" (PA, l. 190). Why, he wonders, "is all around us here / As if some lesser god had made the world, / But had not force to shape it as he would . . . ?" (PA, ll. 13–15). His own pursuit of human perfection has been to little or no avail: "For I, being simple, thought to work His will, / And have but stricken with the sword in vain; / . . . and all my realm / Reels back into the beast, and is no more" (PA, ll. 22–26).

Arthur achieves the partial understanding that it is impossible to create a perfect man and that it is immoral to attempt to do so. For laying one's will on another means robbing that individual of his own volition. As Tennyson himself said, "Take away the sense of individual responsibility and men sink into pessimism and madness."[10] This is exactly what takes place among the knights, for example Balin, Percivale, Pelleas, even Lancelot. Having "bowed the will" (PA, l. 291) of his Order, Arthur has caused the chaos which now surrounds him. And being thus aware, realizing that he has been simultaneously both right and wrong, he is stripped of his "authority" and acknowledges that "on my heart hath fallen / Confusion, till I know not what I am, / Nor whence I am, nor whether I be King" (PA, ll. 289, 143–45).

Brought by circumstance to an understanding of the doctrine

of becoming, Arthur now perceives that "the old order changeth, yielding place to new" and that this is as it should be: "God fulfils himself in many ways, / Lest one good custom should corrupt the world" (PA, ll. 408–10). He, Arthur, had come with the authority of the Absolute to pursue within the realm of the finite the values of the infinite. But in this endeavor he discovered what Schlegel called the "indissoluble antagonism between the absolute and the relative" (*L* 108; *KA,* 2:160). For in light of moral law he had proven culpable in compelling assent to those very values which it was his mission to proclaim. Feeling then, like Nietzsche's tragic hero, both justified and unjustified, Arthur believes himself worthy of reward but doubtful of attaining it. It is right that he now pass on—but to where? To the paradise of Avilion surely. But then immediately he wonders: "if indeed I go / (For all my mind is clouded with a doubt)" (PA, ll. 425–26). In the last lines of the poem he is carried away but to what and where is left ambiguous, as the departing funeral barge is transformed into "one black dot against the verge of dawn" (l. 439).

Much of *Idylls of the King* is ambiguous, indeed indeterminate. First, we can never know the truth of Arthur's birth, whether he is illegitimate or a son of Gorlois or of Uther, or of supernatural origin. As Merlin asks rhetorically, "where is he who knows?" It is a matter of individual perception: "And truth is this to me, and that to thee" (CA, ll. 409, 406). Glossing this passage, Tennyson noted: "The truth appears in different guise to different persons. The one fact is that man comes from the great deep and returns to it" (Ricks, p. 1480n). Second, we can never be sure whether the knights ever saw the Grail or some natural phenomenon. As remarked earlier, Tennyson said that he expressed in "The Holy Grail" his "strong feeling as to the Reality of the Unseen" but then undercut this statement by notes suggesting that the Grail knights were deluded (Ricks, pp. 1661, 1676, 1680) and by having Arthur himself express his doubts (HG, l. 869). Third, we cannot tell whether Arthur goes to paradise or merely disappears into nothingness; that is, we cannot know whether the ending of the poem is pessimistic

or optimistic. Arthur's mind is "clouded with a doubt" as he
wonders "if indeed I go" (PA, ll. 425–26), and Bedivere's account
of what happens is reported in qualified language, in terms of
"seemed," "as," "as if," and "like." As Kerry McSweeney observes, the ending of the *Idylls* "is neither optimistic nor pessimistic; it is indeterminate, offering alternative possibilities."[11]

Adding to the ambiguities of the poem is the light and color
imagery. Light, in the poem usually associated with good, especially with Arthur, is not only illuminating but also blinding,
when, for example, the knights sworn by the King are "dazed, as
one who wakes / Half-blinded at the coming of a light" (CA,
ll. 264–65). The color red is usually associated with sexual indul-
gence, but it is also the color of the Holy Grail. White, on the other
hand, is generally significant of innocence, but the sleeve of the lily
maid of Astolat is red. Tennyson has purposely designed the whole
to preclude our saying positively, as he put it, "*This* means *that*"
(Ricks, p. 1463). Probably the best gloss on the poem is Merlin's
"riddling," carrying with it the veiled sanction of the author:
"Confusion, and illusion, and relation, / Elusion, and occasion,
and evasion" (GL, ll. 281–82).

Throughout, Tennyson appears careful to evade responsibility
for the course of action that his story follows. His narrative manner
often suggests redaction, as though he were the editor of Arthurian
source material, shaping it into proper narrative form. We find this
in the first idyll when the narrator, who had originally seemed
omniscient, continues with the story of Arthur's early days by
saying, "Thereafter—as he speaks who tells the tale" (CA, l. 94).
In "Gareth and Lynette" he alludes to Malory, "he that told the tale
in olden times" (l. 1392). Again, in "Pelleas and Ettarre" he cites
the authority of his source for the narrative, "And he that tells the
tale / Says . . ." (ll. 482–83). In "The Last Tournament" he
apparently refers to a source, "he that tells the tale" (l. 226). In two
other idylls the narrative is given over to other narrators: "The
Holy Grail" is a colloquy but consists mainly of Percivale's relating
of the story, and "The Passing of Arthur" is said, in a syntactically

involved sentence fragment, to be the story told by Sir Bedivere but seems in fact to be a retelling by someone else, for Bedivere is referred to in the third person.

All this appears to indicate an objective narrative without any sign of the personality of the narrator. But this is more apparent than real. To be sure, "he that tells the tale" is, as Dwight Culler suggests, a way of avoiding an authoritative voice.[12] Yet Tennyson also makes it a means of getting the author into the poem. We see this in "Gareth and Lynette" when the narrator says, "And he that told the tale in olden times / Says that Sir Gareth wedded Lyonors, / But he, that told it later, says Lynette" (ll. 1392–93), Hallam Tennyson glossing the first "he" as "Malory" and the second as "my father" (Ricks, p. 1525n). At the beginning of "Geraint and Enid" the narrator—in the most obvious instance of parabasis in the poem, recalling that of Dickens's apostrophe to the lords and reverends upon the death of Jo in *Bleak House*—addresses directly the "purblind race of miserable men" who take false for true and vice versa in this twilight world "until *we* pass and reach / That other, where *we* see as *we* are seen!" (italics added). In "The Last Tournament" "he that tells the tale" is none other than the author himself, for not only is there no source for one of the most elaborate similes ("Likened them, saying. . . ,") but Tennyson glosses the passage, "Seen by me at Mürren in Switzerland" (ll. 226–31; Ricks, p. 1711n). *Idylls of the King* does indeed reveal, as his son said, the poet's "innermost being"; and Tennyson wanted to be sure to impress this "being" on his poem by signing it, discreetly as it were, in the manner of a painter of a picture. Like God, he is both immanent and transcendent, and he is also like God in that he is inscrutable, presenting us with ambiguities, contradictions, and paradoxes.

By formal and stylistic means the author also calls attention to his poem as a literary artifice and thereby to himself as the artist. First, there is the title itself, suggestive not of a work in English but of one in Greek. Few titles could be more scholarly or self-consciously literary. Second, there is the mixture of genres upon which the poem is erected. Worked in the mode of the Hellenistic epyllion, or epic fragment, the poem combines epic, lyric, tragedy, romance, and drama.[13] At times there are even overtones of the musical masque, especially in "The Coming of Arthur," in which form, according to his son, the poet seems originally to have conceived his work (Ricks, p. 1461). Third, there is the gorgeous, ornate style. The exquisite arrangements of consonants and vowels, even in dramatic passages (for instance, "Which flesh and blood perforce would violate" [LT, 1. 684]); the grand rhetorical flourishes like the famous oxymoron "His honour rooted in dishonour stood. / And faith unfaithful kept him falsely true" (LE, ll. 871–72)—what could be more contrived, more designed to impress upon the reader the artificiality of the narrative? Moreover, the style is not consistent: as Tennyson said, the language of the frame idylls is "intentionally more archaic than the others" (Ricks, p. 1742).[14] Fourth, the idylls, particularly the ten forming "The Round Table," become formally more complicated as the story advances, with the cinematic flashback technique used increasingly to suggest disharmony and discontinuity, as though the narrative were making known its own dissolution into the artifice of eternity, an arabesque of the most intricate jeweled work. By all these means the reader is never allowed to forget that here is a "fantasy"—charades, as G. M. Hopkins called them, *Charades from the Middle Ages*"[15]—proceeding from the "fancy" of the poet,[16] who, hovering above his work, acknowledges its paradoxes and contradictions.

7

THE HERACLITEANISM OF
MARIUS THE EPICUREAN

In a note to the third edition of *The Renaissance* (1888) Walter Pater stated that he was restoring the "Conclusion," suppressed in the second edition because "it might possibly mislead some . . . young men," for he had "dealt more fully in *Marius the Epicurean* [1885] with the thoughts suggested by it."[1] Although nearly all of Pater's critics and biographers have remarked on the connection, none has convincingly demonstrated the precise link between the two.[2] In my view it is the idealist doctrine of becoming, eternal change without telos, that informs the novel, which in turn elaborates the "Conclusion," and marks it as a work of romantic irony.

Pater sees Heraclitus, the Greek philosopher of the sixth century B.C., as the avatar of the philosophy of change, his notion of perpetual flux having come to be the dominant philosophical doctrine of modern times:

> The entire modern theory of "development," in all its various
> phases . . . —what is it but old Heracliteanism awake once
> more in a new world, and grown to full proportions? / *Panta
> chorei, panta rei.* —It is the burden of Hegel on the one
> hand . . . and on the other hand of Darwin and Darwinism, for
> which "type" itself properly *is* not but is only always *becom-*

ing. The bold paradox of Heraclitus is, in effect, repeated on all
sides. . . . Nay, the idea of development . . . is at last invading
one by one, as the secret of their explanation, all the products
of mind, the very mind itself, the abstract reason. . . . Gradually we have come to think, or to feel, that primary certitude.
(*Plato and Platonism,* pp. 19–21; Greek transliterated)

Pater's own adherence to Heracliteanism, although understood
imperfectly at first, is reflected everywhere in his works. The
"Conclusion" to *The Renaissance,* originally part of a review of
William Morris's *Poems* in the *Westminister Review* for October
1868, is prefixed by a quotation in Greek from Plato's *Cratylus:*
"Heraclitus says that all things give way and nothing remains."
Here, however, Heracliteanism is mainly a philosophy of *carpe
diem.* "While all melts under our feet, we may well grasp at any
exquisite passion, or any contribution to knowledge that seems by
a lifted horizon to set the spirit free for a moment" (p. 237). Not
the fruits of experience but experience itself, there "our one
chance lies," and so we must aim at "getting as many pulsations
as possible into a given time" (p. 238). In short, the "Conclusion," which in fact had little relevance to the preceding essays or,
for that matter, to the review of which it was originally a part,
expresses Pater's firm belief that this is a world of perpetual flux
in which what is "irresistibly real and attractive for us" is real
"for that moment only" before it fades into nothingness (p. 236).

In the later 1870s and early 1880s Pater discovered, to no
small degree from Browning, that his understanding of Heraclitus's philosophy had been faulty to the extent that he had been
unable to conceive of the flux as being indeed perpetual, not
ending with the individual's life but extending, in some form or
other, beyond the grave to some other realm where, as Browning
phrased it in the "Epilogue" to *Asolando,* the individual is to
strive and thrive "there as here."[3] Whether Pater himself literally
believed in an afterlife cannot be determined,[4] but in *Marius the
Epicurean* he was concerned to show through the medium of

fiction that, given credence lent to the philosophy of becoming, belief in a kind of immortality is—perhaps in addition to being a psychological necessity—a logical sequence. *Marius* thus develops "the thoughts suggested by" the "Conclusion," for in it Pater carries the doctrine of becoming, limited to a kind of sensationalism in the earlier work, over into the field of religion.

"We are all *condamnés,*" Pater wrote in the "Conclusion" to *The Renaissance,* quoting Victor Hugo's *Les Misérables,* "we are all under sentence of death but with a sort of indefinite reprieve" (p. 238). And echoing this in the last paragraph of *Marius* he wrote of his eponymous hero, "He had often dreamt he was condemned to die" (2:223). How to escape the death sentence becomes the central problem explored in the novel; and though apparently framed in Christian terms, the answer is fundamentally a reformulation of the Heraclitean philosophy of becoming that Marius sees as having been perverted by the followers—the Cyrenaics or Epicureans—of the Ephesian philosopher.

Between the publication of *Studies in the History of the Renaissance* and *Marius* Pater had produced his first piece of prose fiction, "The Child in the House" (1878), also about a boy who, haunted by awareness of death, turns his sights from Epicureanism to the "sacred ideal" of Christianity. As Mrs. Humphry Ward noted in her review of *Marius,* "The Child in the House" was unsatisfactory as fiction because its "autobiographical matter" had been insufficiently disguised. What the author needed was a form or manner of presentation that was "more impersonal, more remote." This, she said, Pater discovered in *Marius,* but she also remarked that "no one can fail to catch the autobiographical note" (Seiler, pp. 130, 131).

In her observation of the autobiographical nature of the novel Mrs. Ward was joined by her fellow reviewers and has been joined since by nearly all of Pater's critics and biographers, sharing the belief that, as Michael Levey puts it, "Marius both is and is not Pater."[5] Yet it is not merely that many of the events and ideas depicted in the novel are coincident with those in the author's life, not merely that Marius is a reflection of Pater; it is, rather, that the process of representation is subjected to a still further remove. For Pater not only looks at himself in Marius but also, more importantly, looks at himself in Marius looking at Marius. The novel thus is an example of that self-mirroring of which Friedrich Schlegel spoke when attempting to define romantic irony (*A* 238, *KA*, 2:204); it is like that series of receding images noted in the chapter on *Vanity Fair*.

To Marius the world is the stage for a drama in which he has a part but of which he is chiefly a spectator; which is to say that he is both an actor in and observer of the drama that is his life, or, to put it slightly differently, that he is the active reader of the text of the drama of his life and the witness of the enacted play. What he reads is a text that, in his words, "presented me to myself" and what he sees is, in the words of the author, "a self not himself" (2:173, 67). As a child, "even in his most enthusiastic participation" in the world, he was nevertheless "essentially but a spectator" (1:46). Likewise in Rome he was wont "to conceive of himself as but the passive spectator of the world around him" (1:125). In his experience of Christian worship "he found himself a spectator of this new thing" (2:129). Even on his deathbed he continued to be primarily a witness of himself in action, with feelings "such as he might have experienced himself standing by the deathbed of another" (2:219).

Because he existed "much in the realm of the imagination, . . . constructing the world for himself in great measure from within," his life was "like the reading of a romance to him" (1:24–25). Dissatisfied with the reality of the given text, he is concerned to rewrite it in order to live in "a world altogether fairer than that he saw" (1:45). This meant shaping life into a work of art in which "everyday life" is relieved of "the mere drift or *débris,*" and "the ideal or poetic traits" come to be the sole reality (1:53, 54). "How like a picture!" says the narrator as he describes the setting in which Marius and Flavian lie reading *The Golden Ass,* "and it was precisely the scene described in what they were reading" (1:55). And when Marius eventually meets the author of the book, Apuleius "was come to seem almost like one of the personages in his own fiction" (2:76). Life translated into art, "nothing seemed to be its true self" (1:58)—because it seemed better than its true self. As his aestheticized existence progresses from romance to romance and picture to picture, Marius is ever looking for the ampler art form "which should take up into itself and explain this world's delightful shows, as the scattered fragments of a poetry, till then but half-understood, might be taken up into the text of a lost epic, recovered at last" (2:20). Finally the "ampler vision" is provisionally attained, although, spectator as Marius is, it comes to him and not he to it; and regarding the text in which his life is inscribed, Marius in his dying moments "read surely, now, . . . that his last morning was come" (2:219, 224).

Throughout the novel Marius feels that his life is partly determined and partly free. That is why he regards himself as both the writer of the drama of his life and an actor, a kind of puppet, in it. Projecting himself into the play, Marius is constantly peering into windows and entering through doorways opening onto new scenes.[6] At the shrine of Aesculapius on his last morning there his "special director" lifts a panel permitting the boy to look out onto what "might have seemed the very presentment of a land of hope." This was Pisa? "Or Rome, was it? asked Marius, ready to believe the utmost" (1:40). When he goes to Rome, however, he finds the imperial city disappointing because it does not live up to his imaginative preconception of it. He then enters into new settings in hope always of the "ampler vision." But it is never solely through his own will and determination that he attains other scenes, for he is always guided by some "special director" of his life drama. Though he can envision new settings and new situations, his imagination must be localized or incarnated so that the drama can occur. Thus his various flirtations with religions and philosophies: the religion of Numa is associated with his mother and his home, White-nights; Epicureanism with Flavian and the

academy at Pisa; Stoicism with Marcus Aurelius and the emperor's chambers; Christianity with Cornelius and Cecilia's home.
The roles he creates are nevertheless enacted under supervision
and at the prompting of others.

Let us look at his various roles in different settings and the
roles in which he views others. At White-nights, about which
there is something "spell-bound, and but half-real" and where he
enjoys "the charm of exclusiveness and immemorial authority,
which membership in a local priestly college . . . conferred upon
him," he cultivates the "ideal of priesthood" in his role as hiero-
phant of the archaic religion (1:20, 15, 25). The religion of Numa
was "a year-long burden of forms," its liturgy composed of words
whose "precise meaning was long since become unintelligible"
and intoned by priests clad in "strange, stiff, antique vestments"
(1:6–7). Taking "a leading part in the ceremonies," Marius loved
it as theater, a "spectacle thus permitted . . . on a religious pretext" and stimulating "much speculative activity" (1:8, 9). His
experience of White-nights "lent the reality of concrete outline to
a peculiar ideal of home" and his observation of his mother in this
setting made her "the very type of maternity" (1:22). During
these formative years Marius learns "a lesson in the skilled
cultivation of life," which is to be ever careful of his role and not
to confuse it with others, "to discriminate, . . . select form . . .
from what was less select" and, should anything repugnant inter-
vene, "disentangle himself from that circumstance at any cost"
(1:31, 33).

When he moves to Pisa, the time "when he played at priests"
is past. He becomes fascinated by Flavian, who, "like a carved
figure in motion," was "an epitome of the whole pagan world"
(1:133, 50, 53). Marius turns to something resembling closet
drama, "replacing the outer world of other people by an inward
world as himself really cared to have it." To play any kind of part
"in that outer world of other people, as though taking it at their
estimate, would be possible henceforth only as a kind of irony"
(1:133). It would be a kind of Pirandellan situation, as if a char-

acter in one play were suddenly translated into another. For the most part, however, he acted in his own dream play, at this time "lived much, mentally, in the brilliant Greek colony" of the Cyrenaics, which "hung, for his fancy, between the mountains and the sea," and "had almost come to doubt of other men's reality" (1:134, 169).

He is recalled from this world of fancy by "a vivid personal presence," the soldier Cornelius, whom he sees as the type of "some new knighthood or chivalry" and behind whose dramatic mask he perceives "some secret, constraining motive" (1:169, 170, 232). With his new friend Marius journeys to Rome, where he seems to enter the giant theater of the old pagan world with its "magnificent spectacles" (1:188), pageants, and grand public shows, such as the triumph of the emperor, in which "the world . . . passed by dramatically, accentuating, in this favorite spectacle, its mode of viewing things" (2:199). But once again his role is not entirely congenial, for Marius feels to some degree that he is acting in a play with a brief run. He cannot throw himself fully into his part: aware of its factitiousness, he "feels all the while . . . that he is but conceding reality to suppositions, choosing of his own will to walk in a day-dream, of the illusiveness of which he at least is aware" (1:213).

The other actors on the enormous stage also play their parts. The empress Faustine, "the most beautiful woman in the world" (1:218), is a star, as is the co-emperor Lucius Verus, "a popular figure on the world's stage" (2:30). Marcus Cornelius Fronto, having long played the role of orator, "had become the favourite 'director'" (1:222). The chief player is clearly Marcus Aurelius, who wears the dramatic mask of "outward serenity, which he valued so highly as point of manner or expression" yet beneath which Marius observes "some reserved internal sorrow" (1:190–91).[7] With him "every minutest act was considered" and had "the character of a ritual" (1:192). Although he knew "how to act in union with persons of character very alien from his own" (1:194), he was often given to soliloquy and monologue, either

holding "conversations with himself" or seeming "to have forgotten his audience, and to be speaking only to himself (2:37;
1:201). In his pose of "pontifical abstraction," the world being
"to him simply what the higher reason preferred to conceive it,"
Aurelius watches "impassibly" and seems "indifferent" to the
evil in his midst (1:193, 219, 240). Conceiving, like Marius, of
life as a drama, he speaks of early death as one's not having
"played five acts" although "three acts only make sometimes an
entire play" (1:210–11).

Eventually Marius tires of his part in the Roman theater
mainly because of the limitations of the play and of his role in it.
With his "hatred of what was theatrical" (1:124) he is put off by
the posturings and attitudinizings of the chief actors.[8] Strongly
attracted by Aurelius and his Stoic philosophy, Marius nevertheless comes to perceive that, for all the apparent discrepancy between the mask and the man, Aurelius does not transcend his role:
his mask of detachment is indeed the outward manifestation of his
real indifference to suffering and evil. Startled into feeling by the
cruelty of the public show, Marius sees Aurelius as his inferior
because of the emperor's lack of feeling. And with his altered
opinion of the protagonist in the Roman drama Marius notes a
change in the play itself, a transformation into a kind of Man-
ichaean melodrama in which is enacted "a fierce opposition of
real good and real evil" (1:241). In the new modality Marius will
of course require a new role.

At this point of intermission Marius pauses to take stock of
his own Epicurean philosophy. Cyrenaicism, says the narrator, is
the characteristic philosophy of the young because "the inevitable
falling of the curtain is probably distant." If the young Cyrenaic
does consider the final curtain, he says to himself that the monk
who has renounced the pleasures of life "really acquiesces in that
'fifth act' . . . as little as I . . . ; though I may hope, that, as at
the real ending of a play, however well acted, I may already have
had quite enough of it" (2:18). Marius, however, cannot put the
last act, whether it be the fifth or third, out of mind. At Pisa he

had become a Cyrenaic living in the here and now, but on his way to Rome, when a huge stone from a rock slide just missed him and he felt its touch upon his feet, he dimly recognized that against death Cyrenaicism offers no defense (1:165–66). In Rome itself he sees how the emperor's Stoicism is inadequate in the face of death when Aurelius's son dies (2:56). Further, both Epicureanism and Stoicism are, in dramatic terms, extremely limited in that both are characterized by monologue and a lack of sympathy that is the basis of all true drama. Insisting on a monologic "exclusiveness," neither has the extra dimension of dialogue provided by "complementary influence" (2:19). Based on "loyalty to a mere theory that would take nothing for granted, and assent to no approximate or hypothetical truths," each philosophy demands "the sacrifice of a thousand possible sympathies, of things to be enjoyed only through sympathy" (2:22). Neither Epicureanism nor Stoicism takes account of the world of change and the unlimited possibilities it offers. "The spectacle of their fierce, exclusive, tenacious hold on their own narrow apprehension, makes one think," says the narrator, "of a drama without proportionate repose" (2:24).

It is precisely the dialogue, sympathy, and repose of the spectacle of Christianity that initially draws Marius into it. At Cecilia's villa it was "in a sort of dramatic action, and with the unity of a single appeal to eye and ear, that Marius about this time found all his new impressions set forth, what he had already recognised, intellectually, as for him . . . the most beautiful thing in the world" (2:128). The ceremony was a "wonderful spectacle," the participants "answering one another, somewhat after the manner of a Greek chorus," "like a single piece of highly composite, dramatic music" (2:130, 132, 135). It was the height of drama, all done "in perfect order" and leaving Marius "satisfied as never before" (2:137, 140). Cecilia, with her "expression of pathetic care" (2:105), is herself the incarnation of that sympathy so characteristic of Christianity and so lacking in the Epicurean and Stoic philosophies. Through her and Cornelius, Marius learns that sympathy, which can envision an open, as opposed to a closed, world of possibilities, leads to a larger self, a more engaging role, because those in possession of it "have something to hold by, even in . . . that dissolution of self" that is death (2:183). "In the mere clinging of human creatures to each other, nay! in one's own solitary self-pity," says Marius, "I seem to touch the eternal" (2:184). "Identifying himself with Cornelius," he seemed "to touch, to ally himself to, actually to become a possessor of the coming world" (2:209–10).

It is this access to the eternal, this hope of life beyond the grave, that ultimately brings Marius into the greater drama of Christianity, discovering there the true Heraclitean doctrine of becoming obscured by the Epicureans. Heraclitus had begun with a philosophical irony, namely, that everything is in process of change even at the moment that a viewer perceives it as stable. In "that ceaseless activity" in which all things are "ever 'coming to be,' alternately consumed and renewed," the "divine reason consists" (1:129, 130). As conceived by Heraclitus, "in this 'perpetual flux' of things and souls, there was . . . a continuance, if not of their material or spiritual elements, yet of orderly intelligible relationships, like the harmony of musical notes, wrought out in and through the series of their mutations" (1:131). But over time Heraclitus's teaching came to be misunderstood, and Heracliteanism became identical with the doctrine (expounded in the "Conclusion" to *The Renaissance*) that the individual's momentary sensible apprehension was the only standard of what exists or does not exist; Heracliteanism became in fact the authority for the philosophy of the despair of knowledge. Accepting the debased Heracliteanism, Marius (like the young Pater) became a skeptic, doubtful of anything beyond his own ideas and sensations. "*Life as the end of life*" was his goal, as he sought through refined perception and receptivity "the vision—the 'beatific vision' . . . —of our actual experience in the world" (1:143).

He is, however, never comfortable with the precept "*Be perfect in regard to what is here and now*" (1:145). For the worship of perfection of the moment does nothing to relieve death of its sting. Such a creed of course foresees a "fifth act" and "the inevitable falling of the curtain" (2:18), having, like the dramatist of a *pièce bien faite,* a firm notion of closure; but in its emphasis on the moment, the present action, it puts out of view the play's approaching end. Marius, on the other hand, obsessed by death since his earliest days at White-nights, has borne the last act at the forefront of his consciousness and noted the efforts to promote the ideal of a "secondary existence" (1:21) after the close of the curtain. Thus when he is introduced to Cecilia's villa, he is startled to discover, amidst the plague-ridden Campagna, images of hope "snatched . . . from that jaded pagan world" such as the "escape from the grave" foreshadowed in the tale of Cupid and Psyche (2:103). In Christianity he encounters that "bold paradox" (2:102), that philosophical irony, of a true Heracliteanism that treats death as birth. With its emphasis on continuity, tradition, and community it inculcates the principle of becoming, "the old way of true *Renaissance*— . . . conceiving the new organism by no sudden and abrupt creation, but rather by the action of a new principle upon elements, all of which had in truth already lived and died many times" (2:95–96). Here at last was what subconsciously he had been looking for, "all the lessons of his experience since those first days at White-nights . . . translated here" to this place of life in death (2:97).

Christianity having unearthed for him the principle of becoming that lay hidden beneath Epicureanism, Marius is now moved to reconsider his notions about the drama of his life. Far from being the well-made play, the drama, he sees, is not one of enclosure, where all the loose strands are tied up and all the mysteries are explained in the end.[9] True drama, like "true philosophy," does not display that "complete accommodation of man to the circumstances": it does not show man's attainment of "Truth" because in light of the doctrine of becoming truth is always in process of realization, always in advance of any formulation of it. Rather it embraces the Browningesque philosophy of the imperfect and shows its protagonist maintaining "a kind of candid discontent, in the face of the very highest achievement," and having "the consciousness of some profound enigma in things, as but a pledge of something further to come" (2:220). With this new perspective on dramaturgy Marius is ready for death, which, "he reflected, must be for every one nothing less than the fifth or last act of a drama, and, as such, was likely to have something of the stirring character of a *dénouement*" (2:209).

Almost actively seeking death (and thereby the enactment of the "bold paradox"), he returns to his childhood home, "dreaming now only of the dead before him." As he goes to the family tomb, "it was as if they had been waiting for him there through all those years" (2:204). Marius's circular movement, from leaving White-nights to his return there, does not mean however that the "fifth act" is designed to make the drama circular in form. For, looking back upon his life as but the portion of a play, he experiences a desire to get on with things, "to enter upon a future, the possibilities of which seemed so large" (2:221). The drama is therefore to be figured as linear or spiral in form as the protagonist looks forward to entry into what earlier he had envisioned as "that new, unseen, Rome on high," there, as "one [who] belongs to a system," to join in the communion of those who have gone before (2:11, 26).

Finally the moment of the dénouement arrives. Yet it is not at all like what Marius had anticipated. The "great crisis," he fancied, "is to try what is in us." The agon of the lonely hero "can hardly be one's self" represented there on the stage. What in fact occurs is that when "the great act, the critical moment itself comes," it comes unawares. The " 'great climacteric point' " is passed before one is fully conscious of what one has been about (2:212–13). Nevertheless, having bribed the guards to let Cornelius go and thus having "delivered his brother, after the manner he had sometimes vaguely anticipated as a kind of distinction in his destiny," he "felt only satisfaction" at having played his part so well. Marius's only disappointment with the last act is that, now become a romantic ironist, he is allowed no farewell speech, "an eloquent utterance, on the irony of men's fates" (2:213, 215).

The narrator is concerned, however, to disallow Marius the role of hero: "he was, as we know, no hero, no heroic martyr—had indeed no right to be" (2:213–14). For to the end Marius remains essentially a passive spectator, even of "that mysterious drama" of Christianity (2:218). As the Christian faithful gather around his deathbed and place the mystic bread upon his lips, "his unclouded receptivity of soul . . . was at its height" (2:220). Reflecting upon the doctrine of becoming, the "true philosophy," and hearing the voices of the people bidding farewell to the *"Anima Christiana,"* he passes out of the dramatic text *Marius the Epicurean* into a new, as yet unwritten text, "the tablet of the mind white and smooth, for whatsoever divine fingers might choose to write there" (2:220).[10]

As for the text just completed, the ministering Christians have a different interpretation from the narrator. They hold Marius's death "to have been of the nature of a martyrdom" (2:224), and theirs is the last word. Which interpretation then is correct, the narrator's or the Christians'? The answer is both. Marius was in no doctrinal sense a Christian, his strategem for the release of Cornelius was merely an act of friendship, his death was owing to no persecution but to his weakened condition, he sought no martyrdom and did not believe that plenary grace would be granted those visiting his grave—and the narrator is right not to regard him as any kind of heroic martyr. Yet, on the other hand, Marius did in fact give his life that his friend might live, did embrace the Christian hope of an afterlife, did believe in the Christian commitment to sympathy and community—and the people who buried him were right to regard him as a martyr and his martyrdom, as the church held, a kind of sacrament with plenary grace. The case is indeterminate, an instance of the "profound enigmas in things" (2:220) that Marius, forgoing closure and certainty, had come to regard as characteristic of the world of becoming.

Very little in the novel is definite and certain. To Marius things always "seem." To envisage, to dream, to imagine, "he had always set above the *having,* or even the *doing,* of anything." Vision "was, in reality, the *being* something" (2:218). To the narrator the phenomenal world is a qualified one of "perhaps." Even his own fiction is to him problematical. He is not sure of the thoughts of his protagonist: "The fame he conceived for himself at this time was . . . that of a poet perhaps" (1:47). Moreover, he is not even certain of his setting, asking the reader to "pardon me if here and there I seem to be passing from Marius to his modern representatives—from Rome, to Paris or London" (2:14). For hardly an instant does the narrator allow the reader to forget the unreality of the fictional world with which he is asked to engage. This putative "biography" is, as the epigraph in Greek says, no more than "a winter dream, when nights are longest." It is pure artifice,[11] and to keep his reader aware of it he constantly breaks the fictional illusion. He alludes to himself in propria persona: "the time of which I am speaking" (1:27). He is at pains to invite comparison between the Roman world of the second century A.D. and the modern age: "the new era, like the *Neu-zeit* of the German enthusiasts at the beginning of our century" (1:48). He tells of the documents on which he depends for his fictionalization: "certain of [Aurelius's] letters still extant" (1:221); "a strange piece of literary good fortune, at the beginning of the present century, has set free the long-buried fragrance of this famous friendship [between Fronto and Aurelius]" (1:223–24).

What at first seems a tactic designed to give the fiction the look of realism turns out to have exactly the opposite effect, in that the reader is left with an impression of wordiness and pedantry. Cramming into the novel all kinds of disparate material, the narrator creates an arabesque of fact and fiction.[12] Among the items interpolated are the tale of Cupid and Psyche from Apuleius's *The Golden Ass* in chapter 5; Aurelius's oration taken from the *Meditations* in chapter 12; Fronto's discourse based on his *Epistolae* in chapter 13; the reading from "the composition of

Lucian" lifted from the *Halcyone* in chapter 20; the long colloquy
extracted from Lucian's *Hermotimus* in chapter 24; and the lection
of the Epistle of the Churches of Lyons and Vienne adapted from
Eusebius in chapter 26. Employing a medley of documents, Pater,
like his protagonist "partly under poetic vocation," wished his
invented world "to receive all . . . things, the very impress of
life itself, . . . as upon a mirror; to reflect them; to transmute
them into golden words" (1:180–81). He wished, in other words,
to be mimetic. Yet, at the same time, he knew that there "are little
knots and waves on the surface of the mirror" that "may distort
the matter they seem but to represent." Language is inadequate
for the job of representation. What is called "'common experience,' which is sometimes proposed as a satisfactory basis of
certainty, [is] after all only a fixity of language" (1:138); and
language, essentially protean like all phenomena in a world of
flux, will not suffer fixity.

    Throughout *Marius* Pater tries to make plain that his fiction
is essentially a work of rhetoric, dealing with "the era of the
rhetoricians," when "the work, even of genius, must necessarily
consist very much in criticism" and when "the rhetorician
was . . . the eloquent and effective interpreter . . . of the beautiful house of art and thought which was the inheritance of the
age" (1:152–53). The freshness of the early world has disappeared. Homer could make the simplest incident poetic, could
speak constantly with "ideal effect," but "that old-fashioned,
unconscious ease of the earlier literature . . . could never come
again" (1:101, 56). In these late days, when the burden of the past
weighs heavily on the young writer's shoulder, when in fact there
seems nothing left to do, rhetoric itself having reached the height
of excellence, even Aurelius, "with an extraordinary innate sus-
ceptibility to words—*la parole pour la parole,* as the French
say—despairs, in presence of Fronto's rhetorical perfection"
(1:224).

    With love of words Pater shapes the self-conscious linguistic
construct that is *Marius the Epicurean,* less a believable fiction

than a "reflection," "criticism," and "interpretation" of a certain
period of transition in history much like the age in which the
author lived. Ostensibly mimetic, it tacitly admits to belonging
among "the doubles, or seconds, of real things" (1:13). For ultimately it confesses to be no more than the "golden words" of the
author, who at the end of his fiction has his alter ego read "the
precise number of his years" on his father's mortuary urn and to
reflect, "He was of my own present age" (2:206). That Pater
completed *Marius* soon after his forty-fifth birthday and that his
father had died at the age of forty-five is, as it were, the final
signature of the author who, inscribing himself into the text,
enters into and departs from this work claiming to be—and not
be—fiction.

To be and not to be: this is, in a sense, the essence of the
philosophy of becoming. Espousing it, Pater could shunt aside
forever those unsettling questions about absolutes that immo-
bilized the Cyrenaics and resulted in the despair of the "Conclusion" to *The Renaissance.* Like Marius, who learned that all
embodiments are necessarily imperfect representations of the
thing itself, he could now accept "approximate or hypothetical
truths" (2:22) and, forswearing any idea of "complete accommodation of man to the circumstances," accept, not despairingly
but joyfully, the "profound enigma in things" (2:220).[13] "Heraclitus says that all things give way and nothing remains": the
epigraph of the "Conclusion" expressed the hopeless, elegiac
mood of Pater in the late sixties and early seventies. "In this
'perpetual flux' . . . there was, as Heraclitus conceived, a continuance . . . of orderly intelligible relationships, . . . ordinances
of the divine reason, maintained throughout the changes of the
phenomenal world"; these words from *Marius* (1:131) indicate
how by the 1880s Pater had gone beyond the notion that "Heracliteanism [meant] . . . that the momentary, sensible apprehension
of the individual was the only standard of what is or is not, and
each one the measure of all things to himself" (1:131–32). Because he could conceive of Christianity as a philosophy of becom-

ing, as, in brief, a new form of Heracliteanism,[14] Pater was able to write a fiction in which his hero passes from a pagan despair to a glad acceptance of life and death formulated within a Christian framework. What basically happens is that his hero, like his creator, has graduated from a Darwinian theory of flux to an idealist doctrine of becoming. No longer the de Manian ironist of negativity, he has become a romantic ironist and maybe—or maybe not—a Christian believer.[15]

AFTERWORD
Being True at the Verge

In the preceding chapters I have purposely considered works in various genres in order to suggest how romantic irony is informative of a large body of Victorian literature. Having chosen representative texts, I am confident that examination of other poems, histories, and novels in the manner offered here could easily be extended not only to other works by the same authors but also to those by other writers, Meredith and Clough being two examples that come immediately to mind.[1] For, as I hope to have made clear, what Schlegel called "universal poetry"—literature, in both verse and prose, in the romantic ironic mode—is appropriate for and characteristic of the historical period that recognized itself as an age of transition. To use Schlegel's terms it is "an image of the age" (*A* 116, *KA* 2:182).

The spiritual doubts, anguish, and dividedness of the literature of the era have long been recognized.[2] As a result it has all too often been regarded as essentially melancholy or even tragic, expressive of longings for the certainties of ages past. What I propose is another way of regarding the writings of the great Victorian writers: as acknowledgment and acceptance of contradictions and paradoxes, as an embrace of possibilities. Their stance is that of Whitman, who asks: "Do I contradict myself?";

131

and responds, "Very well then I contradict myself / (I am large, I contain multitudes)" ("Song of Myself," ll. 48–50).

It is not that the authors in touch with the most vital levels of their culture celebrated their liberation from the claims of the transcendent; in spite of their lack of certainties in the world of the actual, Carlyle, Thackeray, Browning, Dickens, Arnold, Tennyson, Pater—none of them relinquished faith in the Absolute, the informing principle in the universe of becoming, although they experienced it in different ways. Rather, they saw that their task as artists was to make manifest in their art the values of the infinite and eternal that their age had lost sight of. "What I want," said Thackeray in speaking of *Vanity Fair,* "is to make a set of people living without God in the world . . . greedy pompous mean perfectly self-satisfied for the most part and at ease about their superior virtue" (Ray, *Letters* 2:309). What Thackeray and the others aimed to be, were, in Arnold's words, "physician[s] of the iron age" who diagnosed accurately, to say *"Thou ailest here, and here!"* ("Memorial Verses").

Yet, as Thackeray commented, "it does not become me to preach" (Ray, *Letters,* 2:354). It was not only unbecoming but also impossible, for the cure to the ills of the age was doubtful. "One of the questions that oftenest presents itself," Carlyle wrote to John Stuart Mill, "is *How* Ideals do and *ought to* adjust themselves with the Actual?" (*CL,* 7:24). Carlyle's problem, as indeed that of all the authors studied here, was the relation of the relative to the Absolute, of the actual to the ideal. And for all of them literature— "universal poetry"—was the means of mediating the dualism; it was, as Browning says in *The Ring and the Book,* the "means to the end" and thus itself "in part the end," the "fiction which makes fact alive" and therefore becomes "fact too" (l. 697–98). Yet, as Browning knew, only "God is the PERFECT POET, / Who in his poem acts his own creations" (*Paracelsus* [1st ed.] 2.648–49). To use the terms I have employed earlier, no human can play the role God plays: He is both the playwright and the superstar. And so Browning and the others question the rightness of their formulations about fact and ideality, undercut their assertions about them, and withdraw to stations above their works where—sometimes with a smile, as in the case of Browning, or with a sad countenance, as in the case of Tennyson—they look down upon their creations.

Carlyle, who self-mockingly began to write *Sartor Resartus* as "Nonsense,"[3] termed the finished book a "Satirical Extravaganza" that nevertheless contained "more of [his] opinions on Art, Politics, Religion, Heaven Earth and Air, than all the things [he had] yet written" (*CL,* 6:396). Browning interrupted Sordello's long discourse on metaphysical poetry to say that if his hero achieves what he wishes, "Why, he writes *Sordello*" (5.619). And at the end of *The Ring and the Book* he allows that his poem is little more than "words and wind" (12.836). Tennyson in his elegy for Arthur Hallam admitted, near the close of the poem, that what he found "in the highest place" was "mine own phantom chanting hymns" (*In Memoriam* 108.9–10). Dickens, who frequently used his own initials in the naming of his characters, insisted that his novels reflected his own experiences. When he first conceived of *A Tale of Two Cities,* he says in the Preface, he had "a strong desire . . . to embody it in my own person." And even when the novel took its present form, "throughout its execution, it has had complete possession of me; I have so far verified what is done and suffered in these pages, as that I have certainly done and suffered it all myself."

Romantic irony is, then, both egotistically sublime and negatively capable. Flaubert, who admitted that Madame Bovary was himself and yet strove for the complete erasure of his personality in the novel, characterized it beautifully: his goal, he said, was "to be immanent in his work as God is in His creation, invisible and all-powerful; to be felt everywhere but to remain unseen."[4] Yet unlike God, the romantic ironist is not all-knowing. He is in fact ignorant: he does not know the way things are, he only considers possibilities of how they might be. His role as ironist is thus a skeptical enactment of his position of ignorance, as he submits to his audience the adequacy of his skepticism for further evaluation. In his search for what will suffice, he always retains the stance of one recognizing that, in Gary Handwerk's felicitous phrase, "ignorance is much harder to maintain than certitude" (p. 173).

Far from being, as he is so often charged, sentimental or despairing, the Victorian writer of the type I have described is tough minded. Speaking of his father, Carlyle said: "*He* was never visited with Doubt; the old Theorem of the Universe was sufficient for him, . . . *he* stood a true man on the verge of the Old." But now, "so quick is the motion of Transition becoming," all is changed, and "his son stands here . . . on the verge of the New, and sees the possibility of also being true there."[5] Like Tennyson's Bedivere in "The Passing of Arthur," the Victorian romantic ironist stands alone on the verge as the old order changes yielding place to new. "All barriers seem *overthrown* in my inward world," Carlyle wrote in 1833; "nothing is to *prevent,* to deter me, but also nothing to *direct.* I pause over a boundless, *unpeopled* prospect; ask how I am to walk and work there" (*CL,* 7:24). He cannot know what the new will bring but at least he, like his fellow ironists, can be "true," as, forgoing certainties, he fronts a world of possibilities.

ABBREVIATIONS

A	Schlegel, *Athenaeum* fragments
BB	Tennyson, "Balin and Balan"
CL	*The Collected Letters of Thomas and Jane Welsh Carlyle*
CA	Tennyson, "The Coming of Arthur"
DP	Schlegel, *Dialogue on Poetry*
Furst	*Fictions of Romantic Irony*
G	Tennyson, "Guinevere"
GE	Tennyson, "Geraint and Enid"
GL	Tennyson, "Gareth and Lynette"
Handwerk	*Ethics and Irony in Narrative: From Schlegel to Lacan*
Haney	"'Shadow Hunting': Romantic Irony, *Sartor Resartus*, and Victorian Romanticism"
HG	Tennyson, "The Holy Grail"
I	Schlegel, *Ideen* fragments

135

KA	*Kritische Friedrich-Schlegel Ausgabe*
Kintner	*The Letters of Robert Browning and Elizabeth Barrett Barrett, 1845–1846*
L	Schlegel, *Lyceum* fragments
LE	Tennyson, "Lancelot and Elaine"
Letters to Clough	*The Letters of Matthew Arnold to Arthur Hugh Clough*
LN	Schlegel, *Literary Notebooks 1797–1801*
LT	Tennyson, "The Last Tournament"
Mellor	*English Romantic Irony*
MG	Tennyson, "The Marriage of Geraint"
MV	Tennyson, "Merlin and Vivien"
PA	Tennyson, "The Passing of Arthur"
PE	Tennyson, "Pelleas and Ettarre"
Ray, *Letters*	*The Letters and Private Papers of William Makepeace Thackeray*
Ricks	*The Poems of Tennyson*
Ryals	*Becoming Browning: The Poems and Plays of Robert Browning, 1833–1846*
Seiler	*Walter Pater: the Critical Heritage*
Super	*Complete Prose Works of Matthew Arnold*
Two Note Books	Carlyle, *Two Note Books: From 23rd March 1822 to 16th May 1832*

NOTES

INTRODUCTION

1. J. S. Mill, *The Spirit of the Age*, intro. by F. A. von Hayek (Chicago: University of Chicago Press, 1942), pp. 1, 2. Walter Pater, *Plato and Platonism* (London: Macmillan, 1910), p. 19.

2. Thomas Carlyle, *Sartor Resartus,* ed. C. F. Harrold (New York: Odyssey Press, 1937), p. 194. Edward Bulwer Lytton, *England and the English* (1st ed. 1833; London and New York: Appleton, 1874), p. 281. Stopford A. Brooke, *Life and Letters of Frederick W. Robertson* (London: Smith, Elder, 1865), 1:111–12.

3. *The Letters of Robert Browning and Elizabeth Barrett Barrett, 1845–1846,* ed. Elvan Kintner (Cambridge, Mass.: Belknap Press of the Harvard University Press, 1969), 2:710; hereafter cited as Kintner.

4. James Baldwin Brown, "The Revolution of the Last Quarter of a Century," *First Principles of Ecclesiastical Truth* (London: Hodder & Stoughton, 1871), p. 279. Henry Sidgwick, "Arthur Hugh Clough," *Miscellaneous Essays and Addresses* (London: Macmillan, 1904), p. 60. John Tyndall, "An Address to Students," *Fragments of Science* (New York: D. Appleton, 1897), 2:98–99.

5. Connop Thirlwall, "On the Irony of Sophocles," *Philological Museum,* 2 (1833):489–90.

6. See, for example, Janice L. Haney, "'Shadow-Hunting': Romantic Irony, *Sartor Resartus,* and Victorian Romanticism," *Studies in Romanticism,* 17 (1978):307–33; Anne K. Mellor, *English Romantic Irony* (Cambridge, Mass.: Harvard University Press, 1980); Clyde de L.

Ryals, *Becoming Browning: The Poems and Plays of Robert Browning, 1833–1846* (Columbus: Ohio State University Press, 1983); Lilian Furst, *Fictions of Romantic Irony* (Cambridge, Mass.: Harvard University Press, 1985); Gary J. Handwerk, *Ethics and Irony in Narrative: From Schlegel to Lacan* (New Haven: Yale University Press, 1985); and Frederick Garber, *Self, Text and Romantic Irony: The Example of Byron* (Princeton: Princeton University Press, 1988). More general studies are Ingrid Strohschneider-Kohrs, *Die romantische Ironie in Theorie und Gestaltung* (Tübingen: M. Neimeyer, 1960); D. C. Muecke, *The Compass of Irony* (London: Methuen, 1969); Ernst Behler, *Klassische Ironie, Romantische Ironie, Tragische Ironie: Zum Ursprung dieser Begriffe* (Darmstadt: Wissenschaftliche Buchgesellschaft, 1972); René Bourgeois, *L'Ironie romantique* (Grenoble: Presses Universitaires, 1974).

7. Citations of Schlegel are, except as otherwise noted, from the *Kritische Friedrich-Schlegel Ausgabe,* ed. Ernst Behler et al. (Munich, Paderborn, and Vienna: Ferdinand Schöningh, 1958—); hereafter cited as *KA.* For the translations I have consulted and been guided by those of Peter Firchow, *Lucinde and the Fragments* (Minneapolis: University of Minnesota Press, 1971), and of Ernst Behler and Roman Struc, *Dialogue on Poetry and Literary Aphorisms* (University Park: Pennsylvania State University Press, 1968). Quotations from the *Lyceum* and *Athenaeum* and of the *Ideen* are identified by *L, A,* and *I* respectively and by fragment number. The quotation here is from *I* 69, *KA* 2:263. It should be noted that Schlegel did not use the term "romantic irony" in his published works.

8. All quotations from the *Dialogue on Poetry* are from the Behler and Struc translation; hereafter cited as *DP.* The quotation here is from *DP,* p. 54.

9. Schlegel, *Literary Notebooks 1797–1801,* ed. Hans Eichner (Toronto and London: University of Toronto Press, 1957), No. 1682, p. 168; hereafter cited as *LN.*

10. Quoted by Handwerk, p. 43.

11. *Schriften: Die Werke Friedrich van Hardenbergs,* ed. P. Kluckhohn and R. Samuel (Stuttgart: W. Kohlhammer, 1960—), 3:314. I am indebted to Gary Handwerk for the observation about the ethical effect of parabasis.

12. Friedrich Nietzsche, *The Birth of Tragedy,* trans. Francis Golff-ing (Garden City, N.Y.: Doubleday, 1956), p. 65.

13. Wayne C. Booth, *A Rhetoric of Irony* (Chicago: University of Chicago Press, 1974). Paul de Man, *Allegories of Reading: Figural Language in Rousseau, Nietzsche, Rilke, and Proust* (New Haven: Yale University Press, 1980), and *Blindness and Insight: Essays in the Rhetoric of Contemporary Criticism* (Minneapolis: University of Minnesota Press, 1983). Søren Kierkegaard regarded Schlegel's irony as "infinite absolute negativity," more or less in the way that de Man regards irony in general; see Kierkegaard, *The Concept of Irony,* trans. and ed. Lee M. Capel (Bloomington and London: Indiana University Press, 1965), pp. 289–335. I hope that I have made clear, however, that Schlegel's irony (like that of the Victorian authors whom I propose to study) is quite different.

CHAPTER 1

1. See Furst, chap. 2, for the development of the term and its applications. As her title suggests, she applies the term only to works of fictional narrative (mainly prose).

2. Those dealing with *Sartor Resartus* as a work of romantic irony are Haney; Mellor, pp. 109–35; Lee C. R. Baker, "The Open Secret of *Sartor Resartus:* Carlyle's Method of Converting his Reader," *Studies in Philology,* 83 (1986):218–35; and Handwerk, pp. 82–90.

3. Hayden White, *Metahistory: The Historical Imagination of Nineteenth-Century Europe* (Baltimore: Johns Hopkins University Press, 1973); John Rosenberg, *Carlyle and the Burden of History* (Cambridge, Mass.: Harvard University Press, 1985), pp. 45–46. Among others viewing *The French Revolution* as an epic are John Stuart Mill, in his review of the work in the *London and Westminster Magazine,* 37 (1837):17–53, and Albert J. LaValley, *Carlyle and the Idea of the Modern* (New Haven: Yale University Press, 1968), pp. 139–50. Mark Cumming, "Carlyle, Whitman, and the Disimprisonment of Epic," *Victorian Studies,* 29 (1986):207–26, sees the work as a "disimprisoned epic" that assimilates other genres to its "epic form"; this view is further expounded in Cum-

ming's *A Disimprisoned Epic: Form and Vision in Carlyle's French Revolution* (Philadelphia: University of Pennsylvania Press, 1988). Among those who see it as a tragedy are James Anthony Froude, *Thomas Carlyle: A History of His Life in London* (London: Longmans, Green, 1884), 1:88–90, and John P. Farrell, *Revolution as Tragedy: the Dilemma of the Moderate from Scott to Arnold* (Ithaca: Cornell University Press, 1980), pp. 215–31.

4. See Mellor, p. 135.

5. *The Works of Thomas Carlyle,* ed. H. D. Traill, Centenary Edition, 30 vols. (London: Chapman and Hall, 1896–99), 2:6. All subsequent quotations of Carlyle's published works are from this edition and will be cited in the text.

6. *The Collected Letters of Thomas and Jane Welsh Carlyle,* ed. C. R. Sanders et al. (Durham: Duke University Press, 1970—), 7:20; hereafter cited as *CL.*

7. Thomas Carlyle, *Two Note Books: From 23rd March 1822 to 16th May 1832,* ed. C. E. Norton (New York: The Grolier Club, 1898), pp. 176–77.

8. The most substantial work on Carlyle's ironic view of history, especially as expressed in "The Diamond Necklace," is Lowell T. Frye, "Chaos and Cosmos: Thomas Carlyle's Idea of History" (Ph.D. diss., Duke University, 1984).

9. White does not allow the possibility of Carlyle's romanticizing history and his simultaneously making fun of it: "Romance and Satire would appear to be *mutually exclusive* ways of emplotting the process of history" (*Metahistory,* p. 8).

10. Reading various memoirs of the Revolution, Carlyle found that "it was all to me like the grandest Drama I had ever assisted at" (*CL* 6:447).

11. Charles F. Harrold, "Carlyle's General Method in *The French Revolution,*" *PMLA,* 43 (1928):1150, notes that of the work's approximately seventeen hundred paragraphs more than five hundred are devoid of historical material but express Carlyle's reaction to events of the Revolution. H. M. Leicester, "The Dialectic of Romantic Historiography: Prospect and Retrospect in 'The French Revolution,' " *Victorian Studies,* 15 (1971):5–17, notes that Carlyle's entry into and removal from the narrative is one means by which the author aims to "inform the individual with the infinite" (p. 7).

12. Mill noted Carlyle's "mode of writing between sarcasm or irony and earnest" and wondered whether it "be really deserving of so much honour as you give to it by making use of it so frequently." Carlyle replied: "I have under all my gloom a genuine feeling of the ludicrous" (*CL* 6:449). *The French Revolution* is filled with puns, many for comic effect.

13. Rosenberg properly calls attention to the fact that the work is not called *The History of the French Revolution* but *The French Revolution: A History*.

14. *Two Note Books*, p. 77.

15. See, for example, Patrick Brantlinger, *The Spirit of Reform: British Literature and Politics, 1832–1867* (Cambridge, Mass.: Harvard University Press, 1977), p. 64; Farrell, pp. 118, 216; and Philip Rosenberg, *The Seventh Hero: Thomas Carlyle and the Theory of Radical Activism* (Cambridge, Mass.: Harvard University Press, 1974), pp. 140–41.

16. See the narrator's final sympathy with Robespierre (4:285–86), who is also regarded as one of the chief villains.

CHAPTER 2

1. *The Works of William Makepeace Thackeray,* ed. A. Ritchie, The Biographical Edition (London: Smith, Elder, 1899), 2:588–89.

2. *The Letters and Private Papers of William Makepeace Thackeray,* ed. Gordon N. Ray (Cambridge, Mass.: Harvard University Press, 1945–46), 3:429; hereafter cited as Ray, *Letters.* The best study of Thackeray's concept and use of time is Jean Sudrann, "Thackeray and the Use of Time," *Victorian Studies,* 10 (1966–67):359–88.

3. Thackeray's conversations with Capt. William Sibourne and Major Francis Dwyer are recorded in William J. Fitzpatrick, *The Life of Charles Lever* (London, Chapman and Hall, 1879), 2:405–15.

4. All quotations from *Vanity Fair* are from the Riverside Edition, ed. Geoffrey and Kathleen Tillotson (Boston: Houghton Mifflin, 1963).

5. Echoing *Paradise Lost,* the first chapter ends: "The world is before the two young ladies. . . . " (p. 18).

6. For the parody of "fashionable" fiction, chivalric romance, and neoclassical conventions, see John Loofbourow, *Thackeray and the Form of Fiction* (Princeton: Princeton University Press, 1964), pp. 14–72. Jack P. Rawlins, *Thackeray's Novels: A Fiction That is True* (Berkeley, Los Angeles, and London: University of California Press, 1974), sees the novel as an attempt to mix dramatic action, satire, and apologue, which is a "formal impossibility" (p. 266). Robert E. Lougy, "Vision and Satire: The Warped Looking Glass in *Vanity Fair*," *PMLA*, 90 (1975):256, agrees that the generic mixture results from a lack of authorial control, for Thackeray starts out to write a comedy but ends by "calling into question the efficacy of laughter as an artistic device." Nearly all commentators on the novel find the generic mixture uneasy, unsettling, and (though they do not all explicitly say so) unsatisfactory. My point is that Thackeray knew exactly what he was doing and remained in full control of his novel as it evolved.

7. The best account of the narrative technique of *Vanity Fair* is Juliet McMaster, *Thackeray: The Major Novels* (Toronto: University of Toronto Press, 1971), pp. 1–49. But see also John A. Lester, Jr., "Thackeray's Narrative Technique," *PMLA*, 69 (1954):392–409. In a psychoanalytical reading of the novel Bernard J. Paris, "The Psychic Structure of 'Vanity Fair,'" *Victorian Studies*, 10 (1966–67):389–410, finds the narrative full of inconsistencies and the whole aesthetic structure incoherent because of the neurotic tendencies of the narrator.

8. Bakhtin's view of the novel as a carnival of figures and voices resisting hegemony is particularly appropriate to *Vanity Fair*. See Mikhail Bakhtin, *The Dialogic Imagination: Four Essays*, trans. Michael Holquist (Austin: University of Texas Press, 1981).

9. Loofbourow comments: "Thackeray's characters are refractions of allusive color rather than instruments of rational insight. They do not think . . . [but] must be pushed blindfolded" (pp. 79–80). Robin Ann Sheets, "Art and Artistry in *Vanity Fair*," *ELH*, 42 (1975):420–31, comments intelligently on the function of acting in the novel.

10. Thackeray allowed that "the unwritten part of books . . . would be the most interesting" (Ray, *Letters*, 3:391).

11. For Thackeray's "ironic use of sterotypical novel-material," see Kathleen Tillotson, *Novels of the Eighteen-Forties* (1954; paperback ed., Oxford: Oxford University Press, 1961), p. 234.

12. For the "ironic inconclusion," see Ina Ferris, "Realism and the Discord of Ending: the Example of Thackeray," *Nineteenth-Century Fiction,* 38 (1983–84):292.

13. "Everything in *Vanity Fair* remains at a distance because between the scene and the reader there always stands, with an insistent solidity, Thackeray himself," says Arnold Kettle, *An Introduction to the English Novel* (London: Hutchison, 1951), 1:157.

14. Cf. Rawlins: "That the novel appears to be about fictional characters in action proves to be an illusion; the novel begins to look like a grand rhetorical machine to bring the reader unawares face to face with himself. . . . [A] trap [is] laid to encourage us to make pure moral judgments which turn out to condemn us, and to leave us to resolve the conflict. There is a joke . . . based on the difference between the way we read and the way we live. We read romantic novels with an easy moral absolutism and live according to a more pragmatic creed. By casting us as the characters of his novel, Thackeray asks us to account for the discrepancy" (p. 13).

15. *Thackeray: Interviews and Recollections.* ed. Philip Collins (London and Basingstoke: Macmillan, 1983), 2:261.

16. See G. Armour Craig, "On the Style of *Vanity Fair*" in *Style in Prose Fiction,* ed. Harold C. Martin (New York: Columbia University Press, 1959), p. 96, and Ann Y. Wilkinson, "The Tomeavesian Way of Knowing the World: Technique and Meaning in *Vanity Fair,*" *EHL,* 32 (1965): 370–87.

17. This point is made by Henri-A. Talon, "Thackeray's *Vanity Fair* Revisited: Fiction as Truth," *Two Essays on Thackeray* (Dijon: Faculté des Lettres et des Sciences Humaines, n.d.).

CHAPTER 3

1. All quotations from Browning are from the *Complete Works of Robert Browning,* ed. Charlotte Porter and Helen A. Clarke, 12 vols., The Camberwell Edition (New York: Thomas Y. Crowell, 1898).

2. For Browning as a romantic ironist, see Ryals.

3. See, for example, William O. Raymond, *The Infinite Moment,*

2nd ed. (Toronto: University of Toronto Press, 1965), pp. 29–31, and E. LeRoy Lawson, *Very Sure of God: Religious Language in the Poetry of Robert Browning* (Nashville: Vanderbilt University Press, 1974), pp. 59–72.

4. Although the resemblances are obvious, I do not believe that anyone has hitherto noted that the machinery of "Christmas-Eve" owes a good bit to Dickens's Christmas stories of the 1840s. As I have pointed out in "Browning's *Christmas-Eve* and Schleiermacher's *Die Weihnachtsfeier:* A German Source for the English Poem," *Studies in Browning and His Circle,* 14 (1986):28–31, Schleiermacher's book (1806) is a Christmas dialogue representing many of the points of view on Christianity that Browning treats in his poem. Linda H. Peterson, "Rereading *Christmas-Eve,* Rereading Browning," *Victorian Poetry,* 26 (1988):363–80, contends that the poem is primarily "about the problem of determining meaning, about hermeneutics broadly conceived" and also (without citing the earlier *SBHC* article) that Schleiermacher's book, which "focused on the significance of the religious event and self-reflexively on the means by which significance can be determined," was a likely source for Browning (pp. 364, 365).

5. See, for example, the *Essay on Shelley* and *Dearest Isa: Robert Browning's Letters to Isa Blagden,* ed. Edward C. McAleer (Austin: University of Texas Press, 1951), p. 220. Like Schlegel, Browning regarded the artist's chief business as the portrayal of the Absolute, putting the Infinite in the finite. Irony is a means to renewed creation of signification of the Absolute, and its goal is to raise the reader's attention from the particular to the Absolute lurking behind it. Since, as Schlegel says, irony is informed by the Absolute which it cannot attain, the result must be that the poet, who "has the sense for the infinite, . . . speaks nothing but contradictions" (*A* 412, *KA* 2:243).

6. See Introduction, note 13.

7. Mrs. Sutherland Orr, *Life and Letters of Robert Browning* (London: Smith, Elder, 1891), p. 436.

8. William Clyde DeVane, *A Browning Handbook,* 2nd ed. (New York: Appleton-Century-Crofts, 1955), p. 202.

9. Philip Drew, *The Poetry of Browning: A Critical Introduction* (London: Methuen, 1969), pp. 205–7, notes parallels between Brown-

ing's poem and Kierkegaard's religious dialogues, especially the *Concluding Unscientific Postscript* (1846).

CHAPTER 4

1. Lionel Trilling, *Sincerity and Authenticity* (Cambridge, Mass.: Harvard University Press, 1972; also his earlier *Matthew Arnold* (New York: W. W. Norton, 1939; 2nd ed., New York: Columbia University Press, 1958). Douglas Bush, *Matthew Arnold: A Survey of his Poetry and Prose* (New York: Macmillan, 1971), p. 24. J. Hillis Miller was one of the first critics to note the essential ironic stance displayed in Arnold's verse, although he did not discern its radical irony: "Arnold is a skillful ironist, but his irony is not, as with the great ironists, turned on himself. Irony, like the stance of disinterestedness, is for Arnold a way of not being swallowed up by the world" (*The Disappearance of God* [paperback ed.; New York: Schocken, 1965]). More recently Miller has come to view Arnold "as problematic and as equivocal, in his own view, as is Wallace Stevens" (J. Hillis Miller, *The Linguistic Moment* (Princeton: Princeton University Press, 1985), p. 43. During the last decade several critics have noted the ironic posture evidenced in some of Arnold's poems, the most notable of these being Alan Grob, "Arnold's 'Mycerinus': The Fate of Pleasure," *Victorian Poetry,* 20 (1982):1–20. However, no one has, so far as I can discover, linked Arnold with romantic irony.

2. Max Mueller, *My Autobiography: A Fragment* (New York: Scribner's, 1901), 1:145. Henry James said of Arnold: "Without his irony to play over its surface, to clip it here and there of its occasional fustiness, the life of our Anglo-Saxon race would present a much greater appearance of insensibility" (*English Illustrated Magazine,* 1 [Jan. 1884]:246).

3. *The Letters of Matthew Arnold to Arthur Hugh Clough,* ed. H. F. Lowry (New Haven: Yale University Press, 1932), p. 135; hereafter cited as *Letters to Clough.*

4. *Unpublished Letters of Matthew Arnold,* ed. Arnold Whitridge (New Haven: Yale University Press, 1923), pp. 18–19.

5. *Letters of Matthew Arnold,* ed. G. W. E. Russell (New York and London: Macmillan, 1895), 1:54.

6. *Complete Prose Works of Matthew Arnold,* ed. R. H. Super, (Ann Arbor: University of Michigan Press, 1960–77), 1:174; hereafter cited in the text as Super.

7. All quotations of Arnold's poetry are from *The Poems of Matthew Arnold,* ed. Kenneth Allott (London: Longmans, 1965).

8. A. Dwight Culler makes this same point in the chapter on Arnold's use of elegy in his fine *Imaginative Reason: The Poetry of Matthew Arnold* (New Haven: Yale University Press, 1966), pp. 232–86.

CHAPTER 5

1. For the development of Dickens's thinking about the past and social change, see Steven Marcus, *Dickens from Pickwick to Dombey* (paperback ed.; New York: Simon and Schuster, 1968), pp. 300–313, and J. Hillis Miller, *Charles Dickens: The World of His Novels* (paperback ed.; Bloomington: Indiana University Press, 1969), pp. 329–32.

2. See Lionel Stevenson, "Dickens' Dark Novels, 1851–57," *Sewanee Review,* 51 (1943): 404–5, and Edgar Johnson, *Charles Dickens: His Triumph and Tragedy* (New York: Simon and Schuster, 1952), Pt. 8, "The Darkening Scene, 1851–1858," 2:741–926.

3. *Charles Dickens: His Triumph and Tragedy,* 2:782.

4. In the manuscript of *Bleak House* preserved in the Forster Collection at the Victoria and Albert Museum there are ten slips of paper recording Dickens's search for a suitable title for his novel published in parts in 1852–53. On nine of these slips the author chose "Tom-All-Alone's" and "The Ruined House" or "Tom-All-Alone's" and "The Solitary House" or variants thereof as the joint titles (or perhaps title and subtitle) of his work. Only on the tenth and presumably last slip did he select "Bleak House" as the name by which his novel would henceforth be known. It is instructive to take note of these tentative titles because they provide a clue to Dickens's own attitude about the conflicting points of view of the two narrators who tell the story of *Bleak House.* They seem to suggest that the author privileged neither of the two narratives. The slips are reproduced in an appendix to the Norton Critical Edition of

Bleak House, ed. George Ford and Sylvère Monod (New York: W. W. Norton, 1977), from which all quotations of the novel are taken.

5. Q. D. Leavis's chapter on *Bleak House* in F. R. Leavis and Q. D. Leavis's *Dickens the Novelist* (New York: Pantheon, 1970), pp. 118–86, is a good example of traditional criticism that, taking little notice of the manner of narration, sees the novel as the expression of a unified point of view. Most recent critics, however, have noted the contradictory visions of the two narrators and for the most part have concluded that Esther's point of view wins out, expressing Dickens's belief that a sick society can be redeemed; see, for example, H. M. Daleski, *Dickens and the Art of Analogy* (New York: Schocken, 1970), and Edwin M. Eigner, *The Metaphysical Novel in England and America* (Berkeley: University of California Press, 1978), pp. 193–202. On the other hand, a few critics find the clashing perspectives of the two narratives persisting unreconciled to the end; see, for example, Peter K. Garrett, *The Victorian Multiplot Novel* (New Haven: Yale University Press, 1980), pp. 59–71, who maintains that "*Bleak House* presents an instance of dialogical form precisely as Bakhtin presents it, an unresolved opposition between 'independent and unmerged voices as consciousnesses' " (p. 30). Another concern of critics since the mid-1960s has been the character of Esther Summerson and her reliability as a narrator; see William Axton, "The Trouble with Esther," *Modern Language Quarterly,* 25 (1965):545–57, for an early example, and Joseph Sawicki, " 'The Mere Truth Won't Do': Esther as Narrator in *Bleak House,*" *Journal of Narrative Technique,* 17 (1987): 209–24, for a recent one.

6. This point is made by Ellen Serlen, "The Two Worlds of Bleak House," *ELH,* 43 (1976):551–66. See also Robert Newson, *Dickens on the Romantic Side of Familiar Things: BLEAK HOUSE and the Novel Tradition* (New York: Columbia University Press, 1977). Taking Dickens's remarks in the preface as his point of departure, Newson goes on to define the novel as a genre as an interplay between the empirical and the fictional or the real and the ideal.

7. I borrow the term from Doris Stringham Delespinasse, "The Significance of Point of View in *Bleak House,*" *Nineteenth-Century Fiction,* 23 (1968–69):253–64, who in turn has borrowed it from Northrop Frye's *Anatomy of Criticism.*

8. On the question of closure in *Bleak House* see John Kucich, "Action in the Dickens Ending: *Bleak House* and *Great Expectations,*"

Nineteenth-Century Fiction. 33 (1978):88–109, who finds that "the Dickens ending never really ends" (p. 101); and Mariana Torgovnick, *Closure in the Novel* (Princeton: Princeton University Press. 1981), who discerns a reductively happy ending to the novel.

9. The question has perplexed many commentators. One of the most ingenious answers—that "these pages" refer to the part of the novel that the reader creates—is provided by Bert G. Hornback, "The Other Portion of *Bleak House*" in *The Changing World of Charles Dickens,* ed. Robert Giddings (Totowa, N.J.: Barnes and Noble, 1983), pp. 180–95.

10. W. J. Harvey, "Chance and Design in *Bleak House*" in *Dickens and the Twentieth Century,* ed. John Gross and Gabriel Pearson (Toronto: University of Toronto Press, 1962), p. 148.

11. J. Hillis Miller, Introduction to the Penguin Edition of *Bleak House* (Harmondsworth: Penguin, 1971), p. 11.

12. Many commentators have noted Dickens's use of theatrical effects in his novels, the most notable being Robert Garis, *The Dickens Theatre: A Reassessment of his Novels* (London: Oxford University Press, 1965), and William Axton, *Circle of Fire: Dickens' Vision and Style and the Popular Theater* (Lexington: University of Kentucky Press, 1966). My concern is different in that I am less interested in theatrical conventions and their influence on Dickens than on the characters' conceptions of themselves as dramatis personae, of their world as a play crafted by a master dramatist, and of themselves acting under the direction of other characters in the novel.

13. On the subject of free will in the novel and also its relation to the structure of the work, see Joseph I. Fradin, "Will and Society in *Bleak House,*" *PLMA,* 81 (1966):95–109. See also D. A. Miller, *The Novel and the Police* (Berkeley: University of California Press, 1988) for a study of Bucket as an instrument of control.

14. *The Letters of Charles Dickens,* Pilgrim Edition, vol. 5, *1847– 1849,* ed. Graham Storey and K. J. Fielding (Oxford: Clarendon Press, 1981), 622–23. Speaking of *Bleak House,* K. J. Fielding, *Charles Dickens: A Critical Introduction* (2nd ed.; London: Longmans, 1965), p. 152, says that "as a novelist Dickens is always what he once planned to be if he could speak to his readers through his own periodical, 'a sort of previously unthought of Power.'"

15. Quoted by Johnson, *Charles Dickens: His Triumph and Tragedy,* 2:704.

16. In this novel Dickens seems consciously to exploit the dialectic

between meaning and contradiction in narrative that has been so much the concern of narratologists. See, for example, Bakhtin, *The Dialogical Imagination,* pp. 289ff; and Julia Kristeva, *Desire in Language,* ed. L. S. Roudiez (New York: Columbia University Press, 1980), pp. 35–63.

CHAPTER 6

1. "Οἱ ῥέοντες" ["All thoughts, all creeds"]. All quotations from Tennyson's verse are from *The Poems of Tennyson,* ed. Christopher Ricks (London: Longmans, 1969). Tennyson's comments on his poems as well as those by his family are, except as otherwise noted, also taken from this edition, cited in the text as Ricks. The titles of the individual idylls of the *Idylls of the King* will be cited in the text by the following abbreviations: "The Coming of Arthur" as CA; "Gareth and Lynette" as GL; "The Marriage of Geraint" as MG; "Geraint and Enid" as GE; "Balin and Balan" as BB; "Merlin and Vivien" as MV; "Lancelot and Elaine" as LE; "The Holy Grail" as HG; "Pelleas and Ettarre" as PE; "The Last Tournament" as LT; "Guinevere" as G; and "The Passing of Arthur" as PA.

2. Stanley J. Solomon, "Tennyson's Paradoxical King," *Victorian Poetry,* 1 (1963):264n; Samuel C. Burchell, "Tennyson's 'Allegory in the Distance,' " *PMLA,* 68 (1953):422. Those holding the first view and arguing for the poem's idealistic design are too numerous to be listed, running from the earliest commentators, such as Henry Alford, "The *Idylls of the King," Contemporary Review,* 13 (1870):104–25, to later critics such as Valerie Pitt, *Tennyson Laureate* (London: Barrie and Rockliff, 1962), and John R. Reed, *Perception and Design in Tennyson's IDYLLS OF THE KING* (Athens, Ohio: Ohio University Press, 1969). F. E. L. Priestley, "Tennyson's *Idylls," University of Toronto Quarterly,* 23 (1949):35–49), was the first modern critic to urge that "the defection of Guinevere is by no means the sole, or perhaps the chief, cause of the failure of Arthur's plans" (p. 36). Notable examples of those expanding on this view are Clyde de L. Ryals, *From the Great Deep* (Athens, Ohio: Ohio University Press, 1967), and John D. Rosenberg, *The Fall of Camelot* (Cambridge, Mass.: Harvard University Press, 1973). The view most nearly like the one set forth in this chapter is that of James R. Kincaid, *Tennyson's Major Poems: The Comic and Ironic Patterns* (New Haven

and London: Yale University Press, 1975), pp. 150–213. While Kincaid holds that Tennyson's irony is expressed in terms of balanced but unreconciled opposites, he is more interested in irony as a form, a narrative pattern coincident with Northrop Frye's "mythos of winter" (p. 5), and further, he concludes that the *Idylls* comes to "a bitter and entirely pessimistic close" (p. 210).

3. James Knowles, "Aspects of Tennyson, II," *Nineteenth Century,* 33 (1893):181.

4. A. C. Swinburne, "Tennyson and Musset," *Miscellanies* (1886), in John D. Jump, *Tennyson: The Critical Heritage* (London: Routledge & Kegan Paul, 1967), pp. 341–42. For studies of Tennyson's sources for the *Idylls,* see J. M. Gray, *Thro' the Vision of the Night* (Edinburgh: Edinburgh University Press, 1980), and David Staines, *Tennyson's Camelot* (Waterloo, Ont.: Wilfred Laurier University Press, 1982).

5. W. David Shaw, *Tennyson's Style* (Ithaca and London: Cornell University Press, 1976), p. 193.

6. See Sir Charles Tennyson, "The Idylls of the King," *Twentieth Century,* 161 (1957):277–86.

7. Reed, *Perception and Design in the Idylls,* pp. 69–70.

8. The poet associates Kay with the autumnal imagery pervading "The Last Tournament": the seneschal would come "blustering upon them, like a sudden wind / Among dead leaves" (GL, ll. 504–5). The poet describes him as "wan-sallow as the plant that feels itself / Root-bitten by white lichen" (GL, ll. 443–44). The description and indeed the characterization of Kay are without counterpart in the source, the *Morte d'Arthur,* although Tennyson does say that "in the *Roman de la Rose* Sir Kay is given a pattern of rough discourtesy" (Ricks, p. 1493n). It is as if Tennyson went out of his way to make Kay a discordant note in this early idyll, an early type of "Tristram the courteous [who] has lost his courtesy" (Ricks, p. 1710n). It has long been noted that the *Idylls* are structured on the cycle of the year, beginning in spring and ending in winter.

9. It is worth comparing what seems to be Tennyson's view of music as the embodiment of the will with Schopenhauer's. In *The World as Will and Idea,* bk.3, the German philosopher defined music as "*the copy of the will itself,* whose objectivity the Ideas are" (*The Philosophy of Schopenhauer,* ed. Irwin Edman [New York: Modern Library, 1928], p. 201). For a study of Tennyson's ideas concerning the will, not unlike

those set forth here, see William R. Brashear, *The Living Will* (The Hague: Mouton, 1969).

10. Hallam Tennyson, *Alfred Lord Tennyson: A Memoir* (London: Macmillan, 1897), 1:316–17. "Free will and its relation to the meaning of human life and to circumstance," Hallam Tennyson says of his father, "was latterly one of his most common subjects of conversation" (idem).

11. Kerry McSweeney, *Tennyson and Swinburne as Romantic Naturalists* (Toronto, Buffalo, and London: University of Toronto Press, 1981), p. 117. Cf. David Shaw: "It is possible . . . that Tennyson never intended to resolve the discrepant features of the poem" (*Tennyson's Style,* p. 222n).

12. A. Dwight Culler, *The Poetry of Tennyson* (New Haven: Yale University Press, 1977), p. 240. Culler also notes that "Tennyson has written an entire poem on King Arthur and his knights without one single instance of magic or the supernatural offered on the poet's own authority" (pp. 34–35).

13. For Tennyson's experiments in genre, see F. E. L. Priestley, *Language and Structure in Tennyson's Poetry* (London: Andre Deutsch, 1973), and Donald S. Hair, *Domestic and Heroic in Tennyson's Poetry* (Toronto: University of Toronto Press, 1981). For a study of Tennyson's use of the idyllic mode see Ryals, *From the Great Deep,* pp. 3–54, and Robert Pattison, *Tennyson and Tradition* (Cambridge, Mass.: Harvard University Press, 1979), pp. 15–39.

14. David Shaw says that "the *Idylls* are, in their wide embrace of styles, Tennyson's most ambitious attempt to resolve the growing conflict between facts and values in post-Romantic culture" (*Tennyson's Style,* p. 222). Few of Tennyson's readers have overlooked or not been attracted by the style of the *Idylls.* Carlyle found the "lollipops . . . superlative," masking the "inward perfection of vacancy" (*Correspondence of Emerson and Carlyle,* ed. Joseph Slater [New York: Columbia University Press, 1964], pp. 552–53). Ruskin felt "the art and finish in these poems a little more than I like to feel it" (quoted by H. Tennyson, *Memoir,* 1: 453). George Meredith saw the incongruity of Tennyson's "fluting": "The Euphuist's tongue, the Exquisite's leg, the curate's moral sentiments, the British matron and her daughter's purity of tone . . . . Why, this stuff is not the Muse, it's Musery. The man has got hold of the Muses' clothes-line and hung it with jewelry" (*Meredith's Letters,* ed. W. M. Meredith [London: Constable, 1912], 1:197).

15. Tennyson's characters are, Hopkins said, engaged in "fantastic charade-playing trumpery. . . . Each scene is a triumph of language and of bright picturesque, but just like a charade—where real lace and good silks and real jewelry are used, because the actors are private persons and wealthy, but it is acting all the same and not only so but the make-up has less pretence of correct keeping than at Drury Lane" (*Correspondence of G. M. Hopkins and R. W. Dixon,* ed. C. C. Abbott [London: Oxford University Press, 1935], p. 24).

16. The word "fantasy" occurs seven times in the *Idylls* and twice elsewhere in Tennyson's poetry, "fantastical" once in the *Idylls* and once elsewhere. "Fancy" as a noun occurs twenty times, as a verb thrice, and as the verbal "fancying" once, far more frequently than elsewhere in Tennyson.

CHAPTER 7

1. All quotations from Pater are from the Library Edition of *The Works of Walter Pater,* 10 vols. (London: Macmillan, 1910). The quotation here is from *The Renaissance,* p. 233. Hereafter volume and page numbers will be cited parenthetically in the text. The original edition (1873) of *The Renaissance* was entitled *Studies in the History of the Renaissance.* The second edition, with the title changed, was published in 1877.

2. Mrs. Humphry Ward was the first to note the connection. In her review of *Marius* in *Macmillan's Magazine* in 1885 she said that Marius, "as a young man, starts in life on the principles expressed in the concluding pages of the 'Studies' " (in *Walter Pater: the Critical Heritage,* ed. R. M. Seiler [London, Boston, and Henley: Routledge & Kegan Paul, 1980], p. 131; hereafter cited in the text as Seiler). Wolfgang Iser's remark on the connection is representative of that of most subsequent critics: the novel "brings to life a decisive feature missing or perhaps even deliberately omitted from the 'Conclusion.' There he had put forward the aesthetic moment as a theoretical guideline for conceiving human life, whereas in *Marius* he spotlights the spiritual problems arising from such an aesthetic conceptualisation of life by revealing the moment as the genesis of longing and anxiety" (*Walter Pater: The Aesthetic Moment,* trans. D. H. Wilson [Cambridge: Cambridge University Press, 1987], p. 141).

3. There is unfortunately no study of Browning's influence on Pater. But for his great admiration of the poet see Pater's essay on Browning in which he reckons "Browning, among English poets, second to Shakespeare alone" (*Essays from 'The Guardian'*, p. 42).

4. Pater's biographers and critics have long disputed the sincerity of Pater's Christianity. The most carefully considered studies of the matter are U. C. Knoepflmacher, "Pater's Religion of Sanity: 'Plato and Platonism' as a Document of Victorian Unbelief," *Victorian Studies*, 6 (1962):151–68, and David J. DeLaura, *Hebrew and Hellene in Victorian England* (Austin: University of Texas Press, 1969), pp. 256–302.

5. Michael Levey, Introduction to *Marius the Epicurean* (Harmondsworth: Penguin, 1985), p. 18. Recognizing the author behind the persona, Germain d'Hangest, *Walter Pater: L'Homme et l'oeuvre* (Paris: Didier, 1961), sees the book not so much as a novel as a "journal intime" (1:333). Gerald Monsman, the most thoroughgoing of Pater's biographical critics, maintains that Pater felt guilt and shame for having somehow caused or willed the deaths of his parents. Pater dealt with this guilt "by a textual sublimation or displacement, exorcising his conflicting emotions through the act of autobiography. There, in the text, the paternal figure, reembodied as any preexisting work or critically conservative dogma, is slain so that the younger, as the autobiographical author of his life, might endow himself with that paternity for which as a child he had insatiably yearned" (Gerald Monsman, *Walter Pater's Art of Autobiography* [New Haven and London: Yale University Press, 1980], p. 4).

6. Monsman remarks: "A representational art that copies an exterior reality rather than mirrors an inner vision is an art of entrapping walls, an art of only illusory openings" (p. 64).

7. It is to be noted that the actors whom Marius most admires are those whose performances seem to be of a reserved nature, as though the actor were keeping something back. The actor, like other artists, must not yield to the impetuous desire to tell all but must restrain himself. Cf. Schlegel's remarks on self-restriction (*L* 37; *KA*, 2:151) cited in the Introduction. Addressing the theatricality of *Marius*, which like most critics he sees as a mere undesirable effect rather than as an organic part of the novel, Lord David Cecil says: "The impression left in the memory by Marius, and the rest of them, is that of tableaux, in which in front of an elaborate and beautiful background are posed figures beautifully and elaborately clothed, but who are faceless, speechless and incapable of

motion" (*Walter Pater: The Scholar-Artist* [Cambridge: Cambridge University Press, 1955], p. 240).

8. Pater himself cared little for the theater: "the dramatic form of literature is not what I usually turn to with most readiness" (*Letters of Walter Pater*, ed. Lawrence Evans [Oxford: Oxford University Press, 1970], p. 203).

9. In all his fictional works Pater carefully avoided closure. Of "The Child in the House" he said: "I call the M.S. a portrait, and mean readers, as they might do on seeing a portrait, to begin speculating— what came of him?" (*Letters*, p. 30).

10. Monsman says that for Pater "any ground of reality will lie not in elements material or spiritual but in the relationship objectively established between them—ultimately for Pater by the text" (pp. 67–68).

11. Cf. Monsman, who maintains that "*Marius* is a novel about the hero's development from a state of pretextual dreaming to the diaphanous condition of artistic exercise" (p. 60).

12. The form of the novel has been of great concern to its critics. "The one artistic fault of the book is . . . the introduction of alien episodes, of actual documents into the imaginary fabric; and these give the effect, so to speak, of pictures hung upon a tapestry," says A. C. Benson, *Walter Pater* (New York and London: Macmillan, 1906), pp. 112–13. This judgment is frequently echoed. See, for example, Graham Hough, *The Last Romantics* (London: Methuen, 1961): The novel's "defect is that Pater found it difficult to fill the larger canvas, and had therefore to incorporate a good deal of translated and extraneous matter" (p. 145). Even Iser, among the most perspicacious of Pater's critics, finds "that at times the novel is taken over by theoretical discussion which evidently cannot be coped with by the narrative" (p. 129).

13. Ira B. Nadel, "Autobiography as Fiction: The Example of Pater's *Marius*," *English Literature in Transition*, 27 (1984):35, says: "The writing of *Marius* became the central autobiographical and literary act for Pater that made it possible for him to pass through a crisis of doubt to the security of self-understanding." Billie Andrew Inman, "The Emergence of Pater's *Marius* Mentality: 1874–75," *English Literature in Transition*, 27 (1984):100–23, argues, on the other hand, that Pater's crucial self-appraisal occurred during the mid-1870s.

14. U. C. Knoepflmacher, *Religious Humanism and the Victorian Novel* (Princeton: Princeton University Press, 1965), p. 222, argues that

in *Marius* Pater "rejected the Heracliteanism of *The Renaissance* by yielding halfway to the morality of his time."

15. In so far as commentators have touched on the question of irony in *Marius,* they have concentrated on the ending. D'Hangest sees Marius's embrace of Christianity as an example of the "ironie du destin, certes, ou de la nature" (1:325). William E. Buckler, *Walter Pater: The Critic as Artist of Ideas* (New York: New York University Press, 1987), agrees that, there being "nothing ambiguous about Marius's end," "the ironies are the traditional irony of fate and the dramatic irony of our awareness of the peasants' misunderstanding" (p. 267). Knoepflmacher finds that the "irony of Marius' passive absorption of this final [Christian] 'atmosphere' informs the novel's entire meaning," the irony residing in the fact that Marius sees Christianity as but another voice to be listened to (*Religious Humanism,* pp. 218–19). Although not using the word "irony," F. C. McGrath, *The Sensible Spirit: Walter Pater and the Modernist Paradigm* (Tampa: University of South Florida Press, 1986), echoes Knoepflmacher in finding Christianity one of Marius's "fancies" (p. 94). On the other hand, Jerome H. Buckley, *Season of Youth: The Bildungsroman from Dickens to Golding* (Cambridge, Mass.: Harvard University Press, 1974), finds "little that is ironic either in Pater's depiction or in Marius's view of Christian faith" (p. 161). Harold Bloom, *The Ringers in the Tower* (Chicago: University of Chicago Press, 1971) is puzzled by the novel's irony: "Whether Pater earns the structural irony of the . . . concluding pages, as a still-pagan Marius dies a sanctified Christian death, is quite legitimately questionable" (p. 182).

AFTERWORD

1. Meredith has in fact already been so considered, in Handwerk, pp. 91–124.

2. See, for example, Masao Miyoshi, *The Divided Self: A Perspective on the Literature of the Victorians* (New York: New York University Press, 1969) and Elton E. Smith, *The Two Voices: A Tennyson Study* (Lincoln, Neb.: University of Nebraska Press, 1964).

3. "I am going to write—Nonsense. It is on 'Clothes.' Heaven be my comforter" (*Two Note Books,* p. 176).

4. Letter of 18 March 1857, trans. from *Oeuvres complètes* (Paris: Conard, 1927), 14:164. Compare this remark with Dickens's (discussed at the end of the chapter on *Bleak House*) about the "shadow" that would pervade the periodical he was envisioning in 1849. For Flaubert's remark, "Madame Bovary, c'est moi," and his aiming at total objectivity in the novel, see Francis Steegmuller, *Flaubert and Madame Bovary: A Double Portrait* (1939, 2nd ed. 1950; paperback ed.: New York: Vintage, 1957).

5. Carlyle, *Reminiscences,* ed. C. E. Norton (London: J. M. Dent, 1932), p. 4.

INDEX

Abbott, C. C., 152
Aiguillon, E. A. de V., Duke de, 26
Alford, Henry, 149
Allott, Kenneth, 146
Approximation, 11, 21, 24, 32, 48, 49, 53, 56, 57, 59, 129
Apsley House, 40
Apuleius, 117; *The Golden Ass,* 117–18, 127
Arabesque, 6, 13, 21, 33, 35, 53, 113
Arnold, Matthew, 14, 60–75, 132; "The Buried Life," 63, 68–69; "The Church at Brou," 66–67; "Destiny," 66; "Dover Beach," 63; "Empedocles on Etna," 65, 67, 70; *Empedocles on Etna and Other Poems,* 66; "The Forsaken Merman," 65; "Fragment of an 'Antigone'," 62, 64–65; "In Harmony with Nature," 63; "Haworth Churchyard," 72–73; "The Hayswater Boat," 68; "Heine's Grave," 73–74; "In Utrumque Paratus," 65; "Lines Written in Kensington Gardens," 63; "Memorial Verses," 132; "A Memory Picture," 64; "A Modern Sappho," 64; "Mycerinus," 62, 63, 65, 66; "The New Sirens," 64; *Poems* (1853), Preface to, 68; "Quiet Work," 63; "Resignation," 62, 64, 65, 69; "Revolutions," 69; "The Scholar-Gipsy," 70–71; "Self-Deception," 63; "Self-Dependence," 63; "Shakespeare," 63–64, 69; "The Sick King in Bokhara," 65; "Sohrab and Rustum," 71–72; "Stanzas from the Grande Chartreuse," 74; "Stanzas in Memory of the Author of 'Obermann'," 68, 74; "Stanzas in Memory of Edward Quillinan," 72; "The Strayed Reveller," 64, 65; *The Strayed Reveller and Other Poems,* 62; "A Summer Night," 63, 68; "Switzerland," 62, 63; "Thekla's Answer," 66; "Thyrsis," 74; "To the Duke of Wellington," 64; "To Fausta," 64; "To a Friend," 63; "To a Republican Friend—Continued," 62; "To a Gipsy Child by the Seashore," 64, 65, 69; "Tristram and Iseult," 63; "The Voice," 64; "A Wish," 63; "The World and the Quietist," 62, 64; "Written in Emerson's Essays," 62; "Youth and Calm," 70; "The Youth of Man," 63; "The Youth of Nature," 63, 69

157